Edward III
Sir Thomas More
Cardenio
The Two Noble Kinsmen

THE GARLAND
SHAKESPEARE BIBLIOGRAPHIES
(General Editor: William Godshalk)
Number 2

GARLAND REFERENCE LIBRARY
OF THE HUMANITIES
Volume 236

The Garland
Shakespeare Bibliographies

William Godshalk
General Editor

Number 1:
King Lear
   compiled by Larry S. Champion

Number 2:
Edward III
Sir Thomas More
Cardenio
The Two Noble Kinsmen
   compiled by G. Harold Metz

FOUR PLAYS
ASCRIBED TO SHAKESPEARE

The Reign of King Edward III
Sir Thomas More
The History of Cardenio
The Two Noble Kinsmen
An Annotated Bibliography

Compiled by
G. Harold Metz

GARLAND PUBLISHING, INC. • NEW YORK & LONDON
1982

Library of Congress Cataloging in Publication Data

Metz, G. Harold (George Harold), 1917–
  Four plays ascribed to Shakespeare.

  (The Garland Shakespeare bibliographies ; no. 2)
  (Garland reference library of the humanities; v. 236)
  Includes index.
    1. Shakespeare, William, 1564–1616. Spurious and
  doubtful works—Bibliography. I. Shakespeare, William,
  1564–1616. II. Title. III. Series. IV. Series: Gar-
  land reference library of the humanities ; v. 236.
  Z8813.M45 [PR2875]   016.8223′3   81-13357
  ISBN 0-8240-9488-3   AACR2

Printed on acid-free, 250-year-life paper
Manufactured in the United States of America

To Mary

and to
Mary Ellen, Betty Ann, Harold, Tommy
Clare, Marie, Cathy
Gina and Terry.

PREFACE

In 1978 Lawrence Davidow, then Acquisitions Editor at Garland Publishing, invited me to edit a series of annotated bibliographies surveying Shakespeare scholarship published from 1940 until the present. Major contributions published before that period would also be included. We planned that each bibliography would be as comprehensive as possible, fully annotated, cross-referenced, and thoroughly indexed. Each would be divided into major sections that indicate the dominant critical and scholarly concerns of the play being discussed; these large divisions would be subdivided if such subdivision might be useful to the reader. The general format would thus have to remain flexible so that the form of each bibliography could reflect its contents. Although the authors would be presented with copies of our "Tentative Guidelines," we rejected a rigorous conformity to a style sheet in favor of humane, scholarly decisions based on individual perceptions and requirements. We desired a fairly uniform series of high quality, but we did not want to stifle creative initiative.

We emphasized that we wished complete surveys of current knowledge and critical opinion presented in such a way that the reader could retrieve that information rapidly and easily. To help the reader sift through large quantities of material, each bibliography would contain an Introduction that would trace briefly the history of recent criticism and research, as well as indicate new areas to be explored, if such areas had become apparent during the author's work on the project. Finally, the Introduction would make clear any special decisions made or procedures followed by the author in compiling and ordering his or her bibliography.

The present volume indicates the comprehensiveness of our plans, for we wish this series to be a complete guide to Shakespeare and his works. The ascribed plays are especially important for the student and scholar. In two of them we see the possibility of

Shakespeare as collaborator working closely with other play-wrights. In the case of *Sir Thomas More*, he was more than likely called in to give expert assistance in an attempt to salvage a faltering play; and in the extant manuscript we may have our only glimpse of Shakespeare at work. *The Two Noble Kinsmen* probably owes its uniqueness to the collaboration of Shakespeare and Fletcher. With the other two plays—*Edward III* and *Cardenio*—we have the possibility that they should be added to the canon, for they may have been written completely by Shakespeare himself. This is indeed a rich area of investigation, and the present volume is a sound guide to this wealth.

W.L. Godshalk
University of Cincinnati
General Editor

CONTENTS

Preface, *William Godshalk*   vii

Compiler's Preface   xi

Introduction   xiii

I. The Plays as a Group
Criticism and Commentary   3
Dates   37
Sources   38
Text and Editions   39

II. The Reign of King Edward III
Criticism and Commentary   47
Date   60
Sources   61
Text and Editions   62

III. Sir Thomas More
Criticism and Commentary   69
Date   101
Sources   106
Text and Editions   107

IV. The History of Cardenio
Criticism and Commentary   121
Date   128
Sources   129
Text and Editions   130

V. The Two Noble Kinsmen
Criticism and Commentary   135

Date   170
Sources   171
Text and Editions   173

Index   183

COMPILER'S PREFACE

This annotated bibliography is concerned with four plays that have been ascribed in whole or in part to Shakespeare by responsible, talented scholars with sufficiently significant show of evidence or argument so that the ascription has been accepted by the generality of Shakespeareans qualified to judge of the soundness of the exposition. The large body of ill-founded attributions (see the Introduction) has been excluded. The four plays, in order of the probable dates of composition, are: *The Reign of King Edward III*, *Sir Thomas More*, *The History of Cardenio* and *The Two Noble Kinsmen*.

Included in the bibliography are all the books, chapters and appendices of books, articles, review articles, reviews and notices of stage productions and a limited number of the more substantial dissertations dealing with the four plays and published since 1930, the year of Sir Edmund Chambers's *William Shakespeare: A Study of Facts and Problems* in which he made an effort to bring order to the jumble of attribution studies to that date.

A few entries dated prior to 1930 have been included, mostly limited to earlier items that were reprinted after that year. These have been entered in the chronological sequence of the bibliography on the basis of the original date of issue. Foreign-language items judged to be readily available to most scholars interested in the four ascribed plays have been included. The objective has been to provide a complete bibliography within the defined limits with sufficient annotation to enable an investigator to determine his or her interest. I trust that a high degree of accuracy has been attained.

The bibliography is organized by play with an initial section listing items dealing with the plays as a group, defined as any two or more, followed by a section each on *Edward III*, *Sir Thomas More*, *Cardenio* and *The Two Noble Kinsmen*. Within each major section there are subsections on Criticism and Commentary, Date, Sources, and Text and Editions. What little has been published on the stage history is included under Criticism and Commentary. Entries within subsections are in chronological order. Full bibliographical data has been provided, falling on the side of fullness where a choice appeared possible, following the format recommended in *A Manual of Style*, 12th edition revised, University of Chicago Press, 1969. Comprehensive cross-references have been provided. In compiling the bibliography I have used primarily the annual listings of Shakespearean studies in *Shakespeare Quarterly*, *Shakespeare Survey*, *PMLA*, *Shakespeare Jahrbuch*, *Year's Work in English Studies* and *Modern Humanities Research Association* with occasional reference to other such lists. The libraries of whose resources I have made the greatest use are Van Pelt and Furness at the University of Pennsylvania, Sterling and Beinecke at Yale University and the New York Public Library. To the staffs of all of them I wish to express my appreciation for their assistance. My wife, whose name appears at the head of the rather lengthy dedication, has not only helped in a practical way by typing—and retyping—the manuscript, by checking errant references and questioning tangled syntax, but has also helped in those subtle ways known only to fellow laborers in vineyards such as this. To her I am most grateful.

G.H.M.
Greenwich, Connecticut
August 30, 1981

INTRODUCTION

In the midpassage of Shakespeare's career as a dramatist the London stationers seem to have discovered that his name associated with a printed play helped to increase sales. The first of his authentic plays on the title pages of which his name appeared were the second quartos of *Richard II* and *Richard III*, and the presumed first quarto of *Love's Labor's Lost*, all issued in 1598. In the case of *Love's Labor's Lost* there is a strong possibility that an earlier quarto was published, because the 1598 title page reads "Newly corrected and augmented *By W. Shakespere*." No copy of such an earlier quarto now exists and therefore we have no information on the date or the contents of the title page. After 1598, with only one exception, his name is printed on the title pages of the quarto editions of his genuine plays.

Earlier (1595) *Locrine* bore the title page notation "Newly set foorth, ouerseene and corrected, By *W.S.*" It is not possible to be certain that the initials were meant to refer to Shakespeare, but if they were, *Locrine* was the first printed play, authentic or spurious, with which he was associated. The initials *W.S.* also appeared on the title pages of *Thomas Lord Cromwell* (1602) and *The Puritan* (1607). The second quarto (1611) of *The Troublesome Reign of John King of England* is attributed to "W. Sh."

His name appeared in full, associated, in that form, for the first time with a non-canonical play, in the first quarto of *The London Prodigal* (1605). Three years later the first quarto of *A Yorkshire Tragedy* (1608) has "*Written by* W. Shakspeare." Nine of the ten plays in the Pavier-Jaggard collection of 1619 (the exception is *Henry V*) are said to be Shakespeare's, including *I Sir John Oldcastle* which uses his full name. *The Two Noble Kinsmen* (1634) has on its title page "Written by the memorable Worthies of their time; Mr. *John Fletcher*, and Mr. *William Shakspeare*. Gent[lemen]."

Humphrey Moseley registered many plays during the Commonwealth at Stationers' Hall including on 9 September 1653: *Cardenio*, *The Merry Devil of Edmonton*, *Henry I* and *Henry II* (or possibly a single play entitled *Henry I and Henry II*); and on 29 June 1660: *The History of King Stephen*, *Duke Humphrey* and *Iphis and Iantha, or a Marriage Without a Man*, with all of which he associated Shakespeare's name.

The only quarto of *The Birth of Merlin* (1662) asserts that it was "Written by *William Shakespear* and *William Rowley*." *Fair Em*, *Mucedorus* and *The Merry Devil of Edmonton* were bound together into a volume for Charles II's library and marked "Shakespeare. Vol. I."

Beginning about 1649 stationers began to make use of blank leaves in new books to advertise other books recently published or about to be published. Some of these advertisements contain play lists providing useful information not otherwise available. Three such pre-Restoration lists attribute plays to Shakespeare. The earliest was published in 1656 by Richard Rogers and William Ley appended to "*The Careless Shepherdess*. A Tragi-comedy . . . by T.G. Mr. of Arts." In addition to several canonical plays, the following are listed as Shakespeare's: *Edward II*, *Edward III*, *Edward IV*, *Leir* and *The London Prodigal*. *Two Noble Kinsmen* is included, but unattributed.

The second such list was issued, also in 1656, by Edward Archer as part of "*The Old Law* . . . By Phil. Massinger. Tho. Middleton. William Rowley." The catalog credits Shakespeare with (in addition to acknowledged plays) *Arraignment of Paris* (or perhaps, because of a possible misalignment in printing, *Arden of Feversham*), *Chances*, *Thomas Lord Cromwell*, *Hoffman*, *Hieronimo* (both parts), *John King of England* (both parts), *London Prodigal*, *Merry Devil of Edmonton*, *Mucedorus*, *Puritan Widow*, *Roman Actor*, *The Two Noble Kinsmen*, *A Trick to Catch the Old One* and *Yorkshire Tragedy*. *Edward III* is listed without attribution.

The third list was issued twice by Francis Kirkman, first in 1661, and reissued in an expanded version in 1671. The earlier of the two was published in *Tom Tyler and his Wife*, and the later was appended to a translation of Corneille's *Nicomede*. In an Advertisement to the Reader at the end of the 1671 catalog Kirkman says Shakespeare "hath in all written forty-eight" plays. He attributed to Shakespeare, in addition to the canon (including *Pericles*), *The*

Arraignment of Paris, Birth of Merlin, Thomas Lord Cromwell, John King of England (both parts), *Leir, London Prodigal, The Merry Devil of Edmonton, Mucedorus, Oldcastle, The Puritan Widow* and *Yorkshire Tragedy. Locrine* is assigned to W.S.; *The Two Noble Kinsmen* to Fletcher alone. *Edward III* is included but not attributed.

The Shakespeare Third Folio was published in 1663 by Philip Chetwind. In the second issue (1664) he printed seven additional plays not included in the earlier Folios: "And unto this Impression is added seven Playes, never before Printed in Folio. viz": *Pericles, London Prodigal, Thomas Lord Cromwell, Sir John Oldcastle, The Puritan Widow, Yorkshire Tragedy* and *Locrine*. The Fourth Folio of 1685 also prints these seven plays. Chetwind must have had some reason for including these seven while excluding the many other non-canonical plays earlier attributed to Shakespeare. Pollard suggested in his *Shakespeare Folios and Quartos* (1909) that he limited the additional plays to those that had been published in Shakespeare's lifetime with either his name or initials on the title pages and had also been credited to him in recent booksellers' catalogs (p. 160).

Abraham Hill in a miscellaneous list of fifty-one plays compiled sometime between 1677 and 1703 ascribed one play, *The Witch of Edmonton* (by Rowley, Dekker and Ford), to "Will. Sh". Robert Scott entered the transfer of "*Eurialus & Lucretia*" from the widow of John Martin in the *Stationers' Register* on 21 August 1683. It is one of twenty-six titles under the heading "Shakespeare," the other titles in the list being those of twenty-two acknowledged and three apocryphal plays, part of a much larger list of plays ascribed to various playwrights. *Eurialus and Lucretia* had been listed in the *Register* on three earlier occasions, on each of which, in Sir Walter W. Greg's opinion, except the first, it was "clearly assumed to be a [Shakespearean] play" now lost.

William Winstanley in his derivative *Lives of the Most Famous English Poets* (1687) credits Shakespeare with "eight and forty plays" comprising the thirty-seven of the canon plus eleven others: *London Prodigal, Merry Devil of Edmonton, Mucedorus, Puritan Widow, Yorkshire Tragedy, Thomas Lord Cromwell, John King of England* "in three parts" (one apparently duplicating the authentic *King John*), *Arraignment of Paris* and two plays otherwise unknown, *Lorrino* and *Oldrastes Life and Death*. Winstanley was notoriously negligent and it is graphically possible that *Oldrastes* is an uncorrected compositorial misreading of *Oldcastle* written in a careless or crabbed English secretary hand. By a somewhat greater stretching of the imagination *Locrine* can be read beneath *Lorrino*. Neither *Oldcastle* nor *Locrine* appears elsewhere in Winstanley's list, although the other five of Chetwind's seven plays are included.

About the middle of the eighteenth century John Warburton, Somerset Herald and antiquary, drew up a list of manuscript plays which he claimed to have had in his possession and at least some of which he certainly had at one time or another. Included are *Henry I*, *Duke Humphrey* and "A Play by Will Shakespear." This last is thought to allude to *The Second Maiden's Tragedy*, the manuscript of which Warburton did have and which is still extant. It includes three apparently successive ascriptions, the third of which is "By Will Shakspear."

With the vogue of aesthetic editing of Shakespeare's genuine plays which began in the eighteenth century and persisted into the nineteenth century came also the practice of searching for his hand in anonymous plays. Of course many were found to be at least partly by Shakespeare. If Archer in his list of 1656 was not the first to attribute *Arden of Feversham* to Shakespeare, Edward Jacob in 1770 did so in his preface to an edition of the play. Collier performed a similar service for *A Larum for London* in 1831. The German enthusiasts Ludwig Tieck and Wolfgang Bernhardi in the first half of the nineteenth century reaffirmed earlier ascriptions of many non-canonical plays to Shakespeare and added new ones. Tieck perceived his hand in *George a Green the Pinner of Wakefield* in 1811 and in a letter to von Raumer dated November, 1821, attributed to Shakespeare fifty-nine plays, the thirty-six First Folio plays, Chetwind's seven (including *Pericles*), an early *Henry IV* and *Henry V*, *Taming of a Shrew*, *Leir*, *Wily Beguiled*, *Edward III*, both parts of *John King of England*, *Satiromastix*, *Merry Devil of Edmonton*, *Mucedorus*, *Battle of Alcazar*, *Arden of Feversham*, *Fair Em*, *Fair Maid of Bristow* and *Birth of Merlin*. Bernhardi also found his hand in *A Warning for Fair Women*.

Richard Simpson in a noteworthy article in the July 1, 1871, issue of *Notes and Queries* first called attention to the likelihood that Shakespeare was the author of some passages in *Sir Thomas More*.

He published an edition of *A Larum for London* in 1872 under the general title *The School of Shakespeare*, noting that "Shakespeare's share need not have amounted to more than a general supervision and direction." With the founding of the New Shakspere Society in 1873 Simpson undertook a general study of apocryphal plays. In the Society's *Transactions* for 1875–76 he published his initial results with a list of "several plays which have been attributed to Shakspere, besides the thirty-seven included in the editions of his works." Among the several are some now considered versions of canonical plays, the seven plays printed by Chetwind in 1664, and *Arden of Feversham*, *Arraignment of Paris*, *Edward III*, *Fair Em*, *Mucedorus*, *The Birth of Merlin*, *The Merry Devil of Edmonton*, *The Two Noble Kinsmen*, *George a Greene*, *The Troublesome Reign of King John* (both parts), *The True Tragedy of Richard III*, the *Ur-Hamlet*, *Titus and Vespasia*, *The Prodigal Son* "attributed to 'Posthaste' (Shakspere), in the version of *Histriomastix* preserved in a German translation," *Sir Thomas More*, *The Siege of Antwerp* [alternate title of *A Larum for London*], *Albumazar*, *The Second Maiden's Tragedy* and *Double Falsehood*. Next Simpson prepared editions of seven plays to be published in two volumes, using again the general title *The School of Shakspere*, which however he did not live to complete, the work being finished by J.W.M. Gibbs and issued in 1878. Simpson considered these plays as only part of the school of Shakespeare, his editions being supplementary to plays published by others such as Dodsley and Hawkins. F.J. Furnivall in a Notice prefaced to Volume I tells us that "Simpson . . . contends that Shakspere either had a hand in, or was closely connected with, most of the plays of his 'School', including those in the present volumes," which are *Captain Thomas Stukeley*, *Somebody and Nobody*, *Histriomastix*, *Prodigal Son*, *Jack Drum's Entertainment*, *A Warning for Fair Women* and *Fair Em*. Gibbs notes that Simpson at first intended to include *The Cobbler's Prophecy* and *The Pedlar's Prophecy* but they were dropped for lack of space. In his Introduction to *Histriomastix* Simpson offers the opinion that the German *Esther und Haman* is the same as the *Hester* played at Newington Butts in 1594 and inclines to the "possibility of its being by Shakspere," as he also does of *Grim the Collier of Croydon*.

Although the New Shakspere Society concerned itself mainly with studies of canonical plays, some effort was devoted to those

Shakespearean plays perceived to be collaborative (e.g. *Henry VIII*). In two papers read before the Society, Frederick G. Fleay reported (1874) the results of the application of his metrical tables to *Edward III* and *The Two Noble Kinsmen*, finding that both are collaborations and in part by Shakespeare. Later, in his *Biographical Chronicle of the English Drama* he assigned *The Two Noble Kinsmen* to Beaumont and Fletcher.

Charles Crawford in an essay in *Notes and Queries* (1901) demonstrated by numerous parallel passages that *Locrine* and *Selimus* were closely linked to each other and that both plays borrowed freely from Spenser, which he considers evidence of common authorship. He argues for Marlowe as the playwright but acknowledges that *Locrine* had been assigned to Shakespeare, and that therefore he may have written *Selimus* also.

A.F. Hopkinson edited a series of apocryphal plays under the general title of *Shakespeare's Doubtful Plays*, including *The Famous Victories of Henry V*. He also published an edition of *Selimus* (1916) (not under the *Doubtful Plays* imprint), which he initially accepts as Greene's on Grosart's authority, but concludes with an elaborate display of the common ground it shares with *Locrine*, which he says is Shakespeare rewriting Peele.

The first systematic study of *The Shakespeare Apocrypha* was published by C.F. Tucker Brooke in 1908. In his Introduction Brooke gives a list of forty-two plays which had been attributed from time to time to Shakespeare by other critics. It is intended to be comprehensive, and consequently the list includes *The First Part of the Contention betwixt the Two Famous Houses of Yorke and Lancaster*, *The True Tragedy of Richard Duke of Yorke* and *The Taming of a Shrew*, which he believes to be earlier versions of Shakespeare's plays. He counts both *Cardenio* and *Double Falsehood*. Even so his list of plays attributed by earlier commentators to Shakespeare is by no means complete. From his list of forty-two Brooke selects fourteen which he says "alone appear entitled" to admission to the select circle of the Shakespeare apocrypha: *Arden of Feversham*, *Locrine*, *Edward III*, *Mucedorus*, *The First Part of Sir John Oldcastle*, *Thomas Lord Cromwell*, *The London Prodigal*, *The Puritan*, *A Yorkshire Tragedy*, *The Merry Devil of Edmonton*, *Fair Em*, *The Two Noble Kinsmen*, *The Birth of Merlin* and *Sir Thomas More*. He offers no detailed explanation concerning the omission of the other plays on his list of forty-two, merely making the general statement that Shakespeare had no part in the construction of any of the doubtful plays but may have acted as reviser or elaborator. He discusses in turn the authenticity of each of the fourteen he prints and summarily rejects eleven as un-Shakespearean, finding only *Edward III*, *The Two Noble Kinsmen* and *Sir Thomas More* worthy of preliminary consideration as being in part by Shakespeare. After further discussion he assigns *Edward III* to Peele and *The Two Noble Kinsmen* to Fletcher and Massinger, but accepts the authenticity of three passages in *Sir Thomas More*: the 172 lines of the insurrection scene, the 21 lines of More's soliloquy on greatness and 136 lines in two parts of the Faulkner episode. There is no discussion of the authorship of *Cardenio*.

With the dawn of the modern era in Shakespeare studies and the emphasis on the importance of external evidence and the dangers of ascriptions based on impressionistic judgments, scholars began to turn away from conjectural attributions. In his monumental *William Shakespeare*, Sir Edmund Chambers swept away the bulk of the earlier speculations, rejecting all plays not included in the First Folio except *Pericles* and four others which he ascribed in part to Shakespeare: *Edward III*, *Sir Thomas More*, *Cardenio* and *The Two Noble Kinsmen*, the evidence for *Cardenio* being weakest since it is lost, while that for Shakespeare's participation in the other three being reasonably well-founded. He believes all four of these plays to be collaborative, as indeed, in the case of *Sir Thomas More*, appears evident. In his magisterial way, Sir Edmund disposes of claims for the other plays with the aspersion that they "now receive little support, and deserve none." His evaluation of the nature and weight of the evidence for Shakespeare's participation in the four ascribed plays is set forth in item 2.

In spite of Chambers's chastening efforts and the modern trend toward conservatism in attributions, critical speculation continues, although usually with a more measured approach. John Masefield, commenting in 1954 on Shakespeare's earliest efforts in dramatic composition, asks if he was the originator and the writer of the scene of the Virgins (5.1) in the first part of *Tamburlaine*. E.B. Everitt argues in depth for the assignment of *Edmund Ironside* to Shakespeare (1954); and Seymour Pitcher advocates at book length (1961) his authorship of *The Famous Victories of Henry the Fifth*. Frank E. Halliday in his *Shakespeare Companion* notes that Shakespeare has been thought to be the "Genius" whom Ben Jonson said had aided him in the composition of *Sejanus*, although most scholars believe it was George Chapman. William Kozlenko in the introduction to his reprint (1974) of eleven apocryphal plays under the title *Disputed Plays of William Shakespeare*, originally edited by Henry Tyrell in 1860, says that twenty plays of Shakespeare's were never printed "including *Edmund Ironside*; *The Second Maiden's Tragedy*; and *The Birth of Hercules*, based on a play by Plautus, which was discovered recently in the British Museum by the German Shakespearean scholar Dr. Dieter Schamp" (p. 5).

Lindley Williams Hubbel in the fourth edition of his *Note on the Shakespeare Apocrypha* (1977) lists seventy-five titles of plays other than those in the First Folio credited to Shakespeare, "a sufficient monument," as he says, "to human folly." Omitting, in addition to the canon, plays that probably are bad quartos of canonical plays, adaptations, forgeries and identifiable duplications (e.g. *Cardenio* and *Double Falsehood*) I count sixty-six different titles, including thirteen not listed by Hubbel.

There has been, as might have been expected, considerable diversity of critical opinion concerning the four plays covered by this bibliography in the half-century since Chambers's *William Shakespeare*. In addition to the question of authenticity common to all four, there are, in the case of each play, other unresolved questions. Few scholars have made any effort to deal systematically with the plays as a group. Most noteworthy of those who have is Kenneth Muir who in his *Shakespeare as Collaborator* (item 20) has addressed himself to the consideration of each of the four plays (and *Pericles*).

Scholarly investigation of *Edward III* has been generally directed toward the questions of authorship and date of composition with limited literary criticism and some discussion of sources. Opinion as to authenticity has ranged from the view of Tillyard (item 13) that Shakespeare had no hand in it—the play was written by a university-educated courtier under his influence—to Everitt's that Shakespeare wrote the entire play (item 15), and Hart's that it is from one hand, either Shakespeare or an unknown dramatist (item 5). Between these poles there exists a substantial consensus that Shakespeare composed the scenes of the Countess episode and that the latter half of the play is probably the work of a collaborator. The most comprehensive discussion of the date of composition is that by Wentersdorf (item 86, and in summary in item 71), who establishes a range from late 1588 to late 1594 based on one item of external evidence and internal references to the battle with the Spanish Armada. He narrows it to 1589–90 from other internal hints and a comparison to *1 Henry VI*. Almost all other commentators date it 1594 in consideration of the entry in the *Stationers' Register* of 1 December 1595. Tillyard (item 13) considers *Edward III* the most steadily thoughtful of chronicle plays outside of Shakespeare and was the first to call attention to the unifying principle—the education of princes. Earlier scholars denigrated the structure because of a lack of unity. Ribner (item 78) calls it a highly philosophical play and views it as a precursor of Shakespeare's remarkable sequence of histories. Muir (item 20) compares the dialog of the Countess scenes to Edward IV's wooing of Lady Jane Grey and finds the *Edward III* episode superior in poetry, better motivated than the sequence in *3 Henry VI*, and more effective in exhibiting motive and character. He cannot accept Brooke's suggestion that the play is Peele's. Before R.M. Smith, Holinshed's *Chronicle* was generally thought to be the principal source of the play, but Smith demonstrated in 1911 that Froissart was the source ("*Edward III*: A Study of the Authorship of the Drama in the Light of a New Source," *Journal of English and Germanic Philology*, 10 [1911]: 90–104). This then became orthodox, but R.L. Armstrong (item 90) pointed out that there are some elements in *Edward III* adapted from incidents recorded by Holinshed that are not in Froissart and others for which no source has yet been identified.

While the vigorous debate of the earlier decades of this century concerning the identity of the writer of Hand D in *Sir Thomas More* has abated somewhat, critics have yet to establish a consensus. Greg (item 16) summarily dismisses the repeated objections of Tannenbaum and Schücking in a note and says that anyone capable of judging evidence accepts Hand D as Shakespeare's, as Bald (item 111) does in a comprehensive review of the case. Nosworthy (item 117), Blayney (item 133), Wentersdorf (item 136) and Bradbrook (item 43)—sometimes adducing new evidence—support the identification. Deutschberger (item 109), Huber (item 123), Hays (item 139) and Ramsey (item 141) express doubts or negative judgments. Important new paleographic evidence was recently developed by Dawson (item 185), who demonstrates that the formation of key letters in Hand D could have led a compositor to interpret *babld* as *table* in Theobald's famous emendation of a passage in *Henry V* (2.3.17), thus strengthening the case for identification of Shakespeare's writing with Hand D. There is, if possible, even less agreement on the date of the original composition of *Sir Thomas More*. Depending on which aspect of the evidence is emphasized, commentators tend to separate into early-daters and late-daters. Scholars who can envisage Shakespeare collaborating with Henslowe's playwrights only during the temporary amalgamation of Strange's and Admiral's just before 1594 naturally favor an early date. Those who find the affinity in his acknowledged works with the 172 lines to be limited to his middle plays settle on a date about the turn of the century. The following list gives the dates of original composition determined by the principal scholars who have addressed the date question (in order of the date of their individual opinions): Sir Edmund Chambers—1593; Collins—1601; Bald—1600; Greg—1593; Nosworthy—1600; Shapiro—1597; Jenkins—1590–3; Partridge—1593–7; Wentersdorf—1592; Blayney—1592; Evans—1590–3; Bradbrook—1595; Lake—early 1590s; Matchett—1600; Jackson—1600. The suggested dates for the Additions are also widely scattered. Serious discussion of the literary and dramatic values of *Sir Thomas More* has been sparse and late in our period. There are three articles of substance and a few comments incidental to the exploration of other aspects of the play. McMillan (item 177) disputes the oft-repeated theory that the play as left to us, because it is badly disjointed from a literary point of view, is unactable. He asserts instead that except for some minor lacunae and a few unresolved difficulties about entrances and exits the action has been made coherent. Spikes (item 137) corrects the impression that the play lacks thematic unity and shows that responsibility is the cohesive idea, social and political responsibility in the early part and moral responsibility in the latter part. Forker and Candido (item 147) determine that the dramatic purpose of the play is the revelation of More's distinguishing qualities—wit, wisdom and an interest in demonstrating his thought by dramatic action. Schütt (item 160) studies the sources in more detail than any other scholar. In a scene-by-scene analysis she finds the principal sources to be Hall's *Chronicle* and the biography by Ro. Ba., with some use of other biographies and Foxe.

Cardenio and its posited correlative, *Double Falsehood*, have received only a limited amount of scholarly attention. Most of the commentary addresses itself to the puzzle of the relationship between the two plays. Freehafer (item 194) brings forth evidence and presents an argument that offers a cogent explanation for that relationship, indicating that the original play was written by Shakespeare and Fletcher in collaboration and that Theobald probably did have one or more *Cardenio* manuscripts now lost. Frazier (item 196) culminated years of research on the same topic with the only book-length treatment of the question, concluding that *Double Falsehood* is the unaided work of Theobald and that he may never have had an old manuscript of any kind.

Most discussed of these four plays—perhaps because it is the most worthy of discussion—has been *The Two Noble Kinsmen*. The tangled authorship question has been much debated with no precisely delineated scholarly consensus emerging. Among those critics whose studies have led them to accept the external evidence for a collaboration there is as yet no more than a broad general agreement, most frequently expressed as, approximately: Shakespeare planned the play, initiated the themes and wrote the beginning and ending; Fletcher wrote the middle. Bertram (item 233) elaborated an argument that Shakespeare is the sole author of the play, but his hypothesis has not received general support and Hoy (item 241) mounted a point-by-point and generally effective frontal attack on Bertram's proposition. A study of song and masque elements in *The Two Noble Kinsmen* and in Shakespeare's romances leads Cutts (item 236) to conclude that the main plot of the play is closely allied to Shakespeare's acknowledged work and ascribes the whole of that action to him. He does not discuss the subplot. Noteworthy support for a collaboration is adduced by Hoy (item 227) through analyses of linguistic qualities in the different parts of the play, and by Oras employing metrical tests

(item 217). Bradbrook (item 43 and reiterated in item 258) speculates that the play was perhaps commissioned to provide a setting
for and to exploit the reputation of a notably successful anti-
masque, a feature of a court masque by Beaumont which is
adapted in the morris dance of the country folk in 3.5. Ellis-
Fermor (item 226) on aesthetic grounds rejects Shakespearean
participation in the play and suggests that the parts not exclusively by Fletcher were also composed by him in collaboration
with Beaumont. On similar aesthetic grounds Mincoff (item 215),
Pettet (item 213) and Proudfoot (item 278) arrive at a diametric
conclusion and reaffirm Shakespeare's presence in a collaboration. In a penetrating analysis Spencer (item 202) discerns two
distinct styles and accepts Shakespeare as the author of part of the
play, the part that displays tired mastery—a poetic success but a
dramatic failure. Critics are not in agreement on who selected the
story and who planned the play. Some surmise with Edwards
(item 230) that Shakespeare developed the plan and started the
action, and that the defects of structure are traceable to Fletcher
who either did not fully appreciate the plan or at least failed to
carry it out. Ribner (item 276), Muir (item 20), Proudfoot (item
278) and Brownlow (item 257) also credit Shakespeare with the
original plan, but Bradbrook (item 43) and Kermode (item 35)
detect Fletcher's hand in the planning. There have been several
illuminating studies of imagery and image clusters in *The Two
Noble Kinsmen*, the most notable by Armstrong (item 207), Hobday (item 27) and Muir (item 20). They find that the imagery is
manifestly Shakespearean. In view of the statement in the prolog,
commentators accept Chaucer's *Knight's Tale* as the principal
source, but Proudfoot, Bawcutt and Thompson (items 278, 280,
260 and 267) point out other sources of elements in the play
not derived from Chaucer.

Stage activity in these four plays has been very limited, only *Sir
Thomas More* and *The Two Noble Kinsmen* having been produced.
Published discussion has been attained by the latter in the case of
nine professional and festival productions and by the former of
one professional, one festival, one foreign, three college and
school productions, and a broadcast presentation of the I11 May
Day scenes (see index, Stage History).

I
The Plays as a Group

I. THE PLAYS AS A GROUP

CRITICISM AND COMMENTARY

1 Oliphant, E. H. C. *The Plays of Beaumont and Fletcher*. New Haven: Yale University Press, 1927. "Plays in which Shakespeare was concerned": No. 39, *Double Falsehood*, pp. 282-302. No. 42, *The Two Noble Kinsmen*, pp. 325-348.

Lists reasons given by critics for doubting authenticity of *Double Falsehood* and its relationship to *Cardenio*: the unlikelihood of Theobald having three manuscripts; the disappearance of all three; the omission of the play from his edition of Shakespeare. The story of the three manuscripts is not inherently impossible. Theobald would naturally obtain all the copies he could. There is no evidence in the sale of his books after his death that the manuscripts either were or were not in his possession. Other old manuscripts have disappeared. It has been suggested that Warburton may have had one or more which were destroyed by his cook. The inclusion of the play in Theobald's *Shakespeare* may have been avoided because it might have interfered with his copyright which was valuable and still had eight years to run. The external evidence for the authenticity of *Cardenio* is the entry in the *Stationers' Register* by Moseley on 9 September 1653: "The History of Cardenio, by Mr Fletcher and Shakespeare." Since this is late it has been doubted, but Moseley although not scrupulously honest is not known to have made any false attributions. The fact that a play of that name was produced by the company with which

both poets were associated and about the same
time that *Henry VIII* and *Two Noble Kinsmen* were
produced supports Moseley. Theobald's state-
ments about *Cardenio* fit in with the objective
facts of production and publication which he
could not have known. Its absence from the
Folios of Shakespeare and Beaumont and Fletcher
is of little importance. Moseley did not have
the play when he published the Beaumont and
Fletcher First Folio and it must be remembered
that *Pericles* was omitted from the Shakespeare
First Folio. Internal evidence is difficult
since the play has been substantially revised
and abridged but there are two recognizable
styles, a new voice (Fletcher's) becoming audi-
ble in 3.3. His work is more readily recognizable probably because Theobald felt it was unnecessary to rewrite it as comprehensively as
the Shakespearean part. Nevertheless there are
lines and brief passages reminiscent of Shakespeare and the themes and their handling in
Double Falsehood are not unlike Shakespeare's
late plays. That the writing of both Shakespeare and Fletcher underlies Theobald's adaptation Oliphant has no doubt.

     The external evidence for the authorship of
The Two Noble Kinsmen--the *Stationers' Register*
entry of 8 April 1634 and the quarto title page,
both ascribing the play to Shakespeare and
Fletcher--is persuasive. Its inclusion in the
Beaumont and Fletcher Second Folio strengthens
the case for Fletcher without necessarily weak-
ening that for Shakespeare. Pope mentions a
tradition that the play is wholly Shakespeare's,
and Steevens notes a playhouse tradition that
he wrote Act 1. On the whole, and in spite of
much debate about authorship, Oliphant is inclined to accept Shakespeare and Fletcher as
collaborators with a doubtful possibility of a
minor contribution by Beaumont. He rejects the
idea of revision and of Massinger's participation,
and accepts Thorndike's advocacy of Shakespeare
as the planner of the play. The interpolated
morris dance borrowed from Beaumont's masque
and the allusion in Jonson's *Bartholomew Fair*
establish the date of composition as 1613. The
revival of c. 1625 indicates that it was popular.

Although the characterization in the Shakespearean portion may not be equal to his greatest, the poetry in the run of the verse, the
compressed and elliptical utterance, the sovereign way that words are bent to his purpose, the
boldness of the imagery and the grandeur of the
thought is Shakespeare at his best. Shakespeare
wrote 1; 2.1 to daughter's exit; 3.1 and .2;
5.1 from line 33, .3 and .4.

2   Chambers, E. K. *William Shakespeare: A Study
       of Facts and Problems*. 2 vols. Oxford: At
       the Clarendon Press, 1930. I: 499-518; 528-
       32; 537-42.

       Rejects the claims of all plays not in the
First Folio for inclusion in the Shakespearean
canon except *Pericles*, *Edward III*, *Sir Thomas
More*, *Cardenio* and *The Two Noble Kinsmen*, all
of which he considers to be collaborative. His
analysis of the four ascribed plays, especially
the authorship, is as follows: he agrees with
most critics that there are two hands in *Edward
III*, the one that is possibly Shakespearean
being responsible for the latter half of 1.2
and all of Act 2 (the Countess episode), and
possibly 4.4, the scene in which the beleaguered
Black Prince rejects successive bids to surrender. He finds the vocabulary, style and
meter like Shakespeare, stresses the three
specific links with the sonnets and *Lucrece* and
concludes that the scenes noted may quite possibly be Shakespeare's. The reference to Marlowe's *Hero and Leander* and the comparison of
the Countess to Lucrece both suggest a date in
1594-5 which is consistent with the general
style and the findings of verse tests. There
is little indication of the identity of the
second playwright but it might have been Peele,
or possibly Greene. The sources are Froissart
and Painter.
       Accepts Greg's assessment of the palaeographic
evidence for identifying Hand D in *Sir Thomas
More* as Shakespeare's as sufficiently convincing
if not conclusive. He independently evaluates
the other evidence and agrees with R. W. Chambers that the political content of the insurrection scene is consistent with Shakespearean

thought; with Dover Wilson that spelling, vocabulary and diction are reasonably Shakespearean; and that the meter is like Shakespeare but
not of the earliest. The vocabulary and diction
of the insurrection scene and the greatness
soliloquy are consistent with Shakespeare's.
Asks "If Shakespeare wrote Addition II (c), is
it not possible that he also wrote Addition III?"
(I: 514). The date and the acting company are
unclear. Tilney was Master of the Revels from
1579 to 1610. The state of Munday's script indicates a date near that of the manuscript of
his *John a Kent and John a Cumber* generally taken
to be 1596, but in fact the play may be earlier
or a little later (but see item 156). The name
of the actor (T. Goodal) in Addition V may point
to an early date when he was with Strange's or
possibly the Admiral's but he was active as late
as 1598, when his company affiliation is unknown.
The anti-alien riots of 1595 which led Elizabeth
to order executions makes it unlikely that any
work was done on *Sir Thomas More* in or after
that year. Chambers leans toward an original
date of about 1593 with the additions undertaken
later, but he finally says the date must remain
undetermined. The company may have been either
the Chamberlain's or the Admiral's.

Since *Cardenio* has not survived, the question
of authenticity, in spite of the external evidence of Moseley's *Stationers' Register* entry
of 9 September 1653 ascribing the play to Shakespeare and Fletcher, is probably insoluble. He
doubts the genuineness of Theobald's manuscripts,
but even if some such manuscripts underlay his
adaptation of *Cardenio* there is little likelihood we could identify Shakespeare's hand beneath Theobald's revision. He is inclined to
accept Oliphant's perception of Fletcher's hand
in some scenes of *Double Falsehood* but doubts
the attribution of specific scenes to Shakespeare. He thinks that Theobald may have had a
manuscript of a genuine old play which may have
included an ascription to Shakespeare, but
since nothing in *Double Falsehood* compels a belief that it was in part by Shakespeare, the
issue remains in doubt. The source of *Cardenio*
was probably Shelton's translation of *Don
Quixote* (1612). The play was performed at Court

by the King's Men during the winter of 1612-13
and again on 8 June 1613, so the date of composition must have been 1612.

Credits the external evidence of the *Stationers' Register* entry of *The Two Noble Kinsmen*
and the title page of the quarto (1634) for the
collaboration of Shakespeare and Fletcher and
finds that the internal evidence clearly supports the presence of two writers. Fletcher's
hand is unmistakable and the metrical characteristics of the non-Fletcher scenes (1.1-5; 3.1-2;
5.1, 3 and 4) agree with those of Shakespeare's
verse in its latest stage. Stylistic features,
other than metrical, are confirmatory. He rejects the various ascriptions of these parts of
the play to Tourneur, Rowley, Chapman, Beaumont
and Massinger. The quarto text is a good one
with elaborate stage directions and marks of
the book-keeper, indicating that the copy was
the promptbook. The Beaumont and Fletcher
Second Folio follows the quarto with only conjectural emendations. The morris dance in 3.5
is based on Beaumont's *Inner Temple and Gray's
Inn Masque* first performed at Court on 20 February 1613. An allusion to Palamon is in Jonson's *Bartholomew Fair* dated 31 October 1614.
Since the borrowing from the masque would be
likely to occur soon after its performance the
date of composition is therefore 1613. The names
of two King's men who were with the troupe only
in 1624-26 indicates a revival. The source is
Chaucer's *Knight's Tale*.

3   **Mackail, John W.** *The Approach to Shakespeare.*
    Oxford: Oxford University Press, 1930. Re-
    print. Freeport, N.Y.: Books for Libraries,
    1970. Pp. 107-10.

    Finds that there is enough in the writing of
    the first two acts of *Edward III* to provide
    grounds for the belief that Shakespeare had a
    hand in its composition. *Sir Thomas More* is a
    play parcelled out, owing to a need for its im-
    mediate production, for transcription and com-
    pleting among five different hands. One of
    them, established with a probability which near-
    ly amounts to certainty, was Shakespeare's hand.
    The three pages of Addition IIc are, on the in-

ternal evidence of style, metre, prose rhythm
and diction, clearly his work. *The Two Noble
Kinsmen*, on the basis of external evidence, is
a collaboration. Much the greater part is unquestionably Fletcher's. What is left is pure
Shakespeare; fragments, indeed, but fragments of
gold. The Shakespearean scenes of *The Two
Noble Kinsmen* belong to the same period as *The
Winter's Tale* and *The Tempest* and we may fancy
that they are the latest dramatic writing from
Shakespeare's pen.

4 Oliphant, E. H. C. "The Shakespeare Canon,"
     The Quarterly Review, 259: 513, 514 (July and
     October, 1932): 32-48.

     Appeals for open-mindedness on the part of
scholars in regard to the Shakespeare canon.
The accepted canon of thirty-seven plays may be
incomplete and at the same time may within individual plays contain elements not written by
Shakespeare. Oliphant advocates serious consideration of the admission of *Edward III* and
The Two Noble Kinsmen to the canon because substantial portions at least of both plays were
written by Shakespeare. *Sir Thomas More* and
Double Falsehood should be included in complete
editions of Shakespeare so that everything
should find a place. Perhaps also parts of
The Birth of Merlin and the earlier additions
to *The Spanish Tragedy* are Shakespeare's.

5 Hart, Alfred. *Shakespeare and the Homilies*.
     Melbourne: Melbourne University Press, 1934.
     Reprint. New York: Octagon, 1970. Chap. 4,
     "The Vocabulary of *Edward III*," pp. 219-41.
     Chap. 5, "Shakespeare and the Vocabulary of
     The Two Noble Kinsmen," pp. 242-56.

     Presents statistical studies of the vocabu-
lary of *Edward III* such as comparisons of the
total number of words in plays of comparable
line-length, statistical measures of common
vocabulary in different plays, frequency of
occurrence of words having certain prefixes or
suffixes in different plays, and the frequency
of compound words. Hart shows that the vocab-

ularies of Peele, Greene and Marlowe are meas-
urably different from that exhibited in *Edward
III* while Shakespeare's vocabulary based on
statistical counts from the *Henry VI* plays,
Richard II, King John, 1 Henry IV, 2 Henry IV
and *Henry V* matches that of *Edward III* very
closely. Critics are right to accept the Countess scenes as Shakespearean; but further the
vocabulary of the rest of *Edward III* is much
closer to that of the Countess sequence and to
the acknowledged Shakespearean vocabulary than
Peele's, Greene's or Marlowe's.

Studies statistical occurrence of words rare
or previously unused in Shakespeare's late plays,
words new to literature, compound words, use of
substantives as verbs, words having the prefixes
un and *dis*, and words formed by the use of suffixes not previously adopted in *-like, -ance*
and *-ment* and makes a series of comparisons to
Two Noble Kinsmen A and B, A being all of Act 1,
3.1, and 5.1, .3 and .4, which seems to have an
affinity to the language and verse of *Coriolanus,
Antony and Cleopatra, Winter's Tale* and *Tempest,*
while B--the rest of *Two Noble Kinsmen*--does not.
There is a high degree of statistical correspondence of part A to canonical late Shakespearean
plays while part B shows without exception a low
to very low degree of correspondence. Hart
bases his conclusions on the absence of typi-
cally and statistically Shakespearean vocabulary
from part B and submits that his evidence supports the claim of *The Two Noble Kinsmen* to be
included in the Shakespearean canon.

6 Parrott, Thomas M. *William Shakespeare: A Handbook.* New York: Scribner's, 1934. Pp. 181-3.

Concludes that Shakespeare's authorship of
Edward III based on the "lilies" line from
Sonnet 94 is not proved. Shakespeare is the
author of *Sir Thomas More* Addition IIc on the
authority of a study of the handwriting, the
Shakespearean quality of the humorous sympathy
with the unruly mob, and the insistence on
order and authority. Shakespeare's course as a
playwright was run before he collaborated with
Fletcher on *Henry VIII* and *The Two Noble Kinsmen*

in which is found some lofty poetry.

7   Sharpe, Robert Boies. *The Real War of the
     Theaters: Shakespeare's Fellows in Rivalry
     with the Admiral's Men, 1594-1603.* New
     York: The Modern Language Association of
     America, 1935. Pp. 27, 39, 91, 101, 112,
     117, 143, 176, 238.

     Concludes that *Edward III* is likely to have
been a Chamberlain's play because of the passages which, if not Shakespeare's, are in his
style, and because of the line found in Sonnet
94. Sharpe is not convinced of the date of
c. 1589 suggested by Farmer (item 87), but the
style does not absolutely belie it. Because of
its length and the distinct break at the change
of scene to France, marked by the large type in
the quarto of 1596 (sig. E1^V), Sharpe thinks
that the play was really in two parts. Shakespeare was familiar with *Edward III* as indicated
by the many reminiscences of it in *Henry IV* and
Henry V, which he lists. He regards the Admiral's play *Alice Pierce* as an emulation of *Edward
III*, and notes its anti-Scottish elements.
     Sir Thomas More seems to belong in author-
ship, general tone and social sympathies to
Pembroke's or Admiral's. Sharpe would be very
much surprised to see it proved that Shakespeare
had anything to do with it, unless his share
belongs to the days before the organization of
the Chamberlain's men. Brief passing references
are made to *Cardenio* (p. 29), and to *The Two
Noble Kinsmen* (pp. 40-1).

8   Maxwell, Baldwin. *Studies in Beaumont, Fletcher,
     and Massinger.* Chapel Hill: University of
     North Carolina Press, 1939. Reprint. New
     York: Octagon, 1974. Pp. 54, 56-7, 177-8,
     192.

     Examines the evidence for collaboration be-
tween Shakespeare and Fletcher in *Henry VIII*,
The Two Noble Kinsmen and *Cardenio*. Decides
that there is no trustworthy external evidence,
and that the internal evidence is slight in
The Two Noble Kinsmen, less in *Henry VIII* and

of course none in the lost *Cardenio*. The identification of *Cardenio* with *A Very Woman* is
based on a similarity in the names of the pro-
tagonists in the two plays and is rejected as
"unlikely" (p. 177).

9 Spencer, Hazelton. *The Art and Life of William
    Shakespeare*. New York: Harcourt, 1940.
    Pp. 378-82, 412-5 (n. 4 to chap. 11).

    Cites general scholarly opinion against the
authenticity of most of the apocryphal plays
including *Edward III*. Spencer reviews findings
of Pollard *et al.* in *Shakespeare's Hand in the
Play of Sir Thomas More* and those of Tannenbaum
in opposition and concludes that since the
samples of Shakespeare's handwriting are so few
and the penmanship of Hand D is so normal for
the time that the burden of proof that Addition
IIc is in Shakespeare's hand has not been sustained. From a literary point of view the three
pages might well be his, but Shakespeare had
no monopoly on the sentiments expressed in the
speech to the rebels. On the whole, the chances
are against the addition being his. That
Double Falsehood is an adaptation of *Cardenio*
is implausible. Efforts to distinguish the
collaborators are unlikely to succeed since the
surviving text is adapted. The failure of
Theobald to print the original play and the loss
of his manuscripts casts doubt on his assertions.
Perhaps he had an old manuscript which he
thought was Shakespeare's. The question is
still open.
    The only external evidence of Shakespeare's
participation in *The Two Noble Kinsmen* is the
title-page of the quarto (1634). Against that
is its absence from the Shakespeare First Folio,
its inclusion in the Beaumont and Fletcher
Second Folio, and the *Stationers' Register* entry
of 31 October 1646, transferring title to the
play, in which it is ascribed to Fletcher alone.
These considerations are not decisive and there
is agreement that part of *The Two Noble Kinsmen*
is Shakespeare's, which is supported by the
strong probability that Shakespeare and Fletcher
collaborated in *Henry VIII* and *Cardenio*. To

Shakespeare may fairly confidently be assigned
1.1 (except the opening song), .2, .3 and
.4; 2.1; 3.1; 4.3; and 5.1, .3 and .4. The
author of the prolog and epilog, which may be
later than the play, is unknown. Spencer
entertains the notion that every scene may be a
joint effort and that the collaborators revised
each other's work. In *The Two Noble Kinsmen*
there is almost no poetry, less characterization
and many spectacular effects. Shakespeare's
best contribution (the prayers to the gods) is
not dramatic. The tone of the piece is
Fletcher's. The only interest is which of the
knightly cousins will draw which destiny.
There is a kind of grim propriety in the imperfections of *The Two Noble Kinsmen,* Shakespeare's final work. It smells of mortality.

10   Chambrum, Clara Longworth de. *Shakespeare: A
        Portrait Restored.* London: Hollis & Carter,
        1957. Originally published in French under
        the title *Shakespeare Retrouvé: Sa vie; son
        oeuvre.* Paris: Larousse/Plon, 1947. Trans-
        lated by the author. Pp. 71-2, 74-5, 156,
        326, 353, 363.

        Concludes that Shakespeare and Marlowe col-
        laborated on *Edward III* as they did on *Edward
        II* and the *Henry VI* trilogy. Reiterates her
        views on *Sir Thomas More* as set forth in item
        104. *Cardenio, The Two Noble Kinsmen* and *Henry
        VIII* were collaborations of Shakespeare and
        Fletcher.

11   Bentley, Gerald Eades. "Shakespeare and the
        Blackfriars Theatre," *Shakespeare Survey,* 1
        (1948): 38-50. Reprint. *Shakespeare and
        His Theatre.* Lincoln: University of
        Nebraska Press, 1964; and in *The Two Noble
        Kinsmen* edited by Clifford Leech, *Signet
        Classic Shakespeare*, 3d **ed., rev.** 1977.

        Recognizes (along with *Cymbeline, Winter's
        Tale* and *Tempest*) *Cardenio* and *Two Noble Kinsmen*
        as plays written especially to appeal to the
        courtly, more sophisticated audiences at the
        private Blackfriars Theater. Concludes that

Cardenio and *The Two Noble Kinsmen*, along with
Henry VIII, were written by Shakespeare in
collaboration with Fletcher and were equally
as successful as his earlier romances and
Philaster (in which Shakespeare did not par-
ticipate) are known to have been.

12   Brooke, C. F. Tucker.   "The Renaissance."   *A*
       Literary History of England.   Edited by
       Albert C. Baugh.   New York: Appleton-Century-
       Crofts, 1948.   Pp. 315-696.

       Acquiesces in the assignment of part of *Sir*
Thomas More to Shakespeare and to the collaboration of Shakespeare and Fletcher in *The Two*
Noble Kinsmen.   Brooke revises his view of
Shakespearean participation in *Edward III*
originally set forth in item 50 and now finds
good reasons for seeing Shakespeare's hand in
the play (p. 468).

13   Tillyard, E. M. W.   *Shakespeare's History Plays*.
       London: Chatto & Windus, 1948.   Pp. 106,
       109-14, 120-2, 162-3.

       Finds that *Edward III* and *Sir Thomas More*
stand out as clearly superior to the norm of
early chronicle plays in exhibiting (along with
Edward II and *Oldcastle*) a philosophy of history
and a unifying theme.   In *Edward III* he believes
the theme to be the proper education of princes
and in *Sir Thomas More* the reflection in More's
career of broad political processes with emphasis on the traditional Elizabethan notion of
degree.   *Edward III* is one of the most academic
and intellectual of the chronicle plays.   Warwick's arguments on both sides of his daughter's
answer to Edward show training in university
disputation and Senecan morality.   The author
shows an awareness of cosmic correspondences
(e.g.:   heaven and the body politic) and many
of the figures are academic in origin.   The
question of the bounds of obedience to the
sovereign, explored in the Villiers-Salisbury
incident, is one example of political reflect-
iveness.   *Edward III* is one of the most thoughtful of the chronicle plays outside Shakespeare.

The central theme, the education of King
Edward and the Black Prince, and the vocabulary studies of Hart (item 5) strengthen the
case for single authorship but it cannot have
been Shakespeare, because if it were, its
absence from the First Folio is unthinkable.
The author was probably a young intellectual
with a university education who was one of the
Southampton circle and deeply under the influence of Shakespeare. *Sir Thomas More* is unusually thoughtful for a chronicle play as
demonstrated in discussions of international
relations and the obligation of counsellors to
inform the king of unfavorable developments.
It is highly probable that Shakespeare was the
author of the 172 lines of the insurrection
scene and of the twenty-one lines comprising
More's soliloquy on greatness. Affinities in
Sir Thomas More with Shakespeare's other work
and the general tone of charm, humor and tolerance lead Tillyard to the idea that Shakespeare
was directing or helping a team of playwrights
and infected them with his own spirit. When
trouble with the censor developed he helped
further by writing two scenes. The presence of
a prevailing political philosophy in these two
plays and its Shakespearean nature demonstrate
Shakespeare's influence on the chronicle play.
Tillyard finds it difficult "to resist the conclusion that Shakespeare was mainly responsible
for giving the chronicle plays any superior
thoughtfulness or sophistication they may contain" (p. 120).

14   Reese, M. M. *Shakespeare: His World & His Work*.
      London: Arnold, 1953. 2nd ed., rev. London:
      St. Martin's, 1980. Pp. 193-8.

      Finds that Shakespeare rarely took part in a
collaborative effort, although he certainly revised the work of other men as in *Henry VI,
Richard III, Taming of the Shrew, Henry V, King
John, Hamlet* and *Lear* and perhaps others. It
is possible that *Timon* was completed by another
hand from an unfinished Shakespearean draft and
that Shakespeare completed someone else's work
in *Pericles*. It is also possible that in *Henry*

VIII, *Two Noble Kinsmen* and *Cardenio* we may
have Shakespearean collaboration because of the
circumstances that he retired to Stratford at
about the time the plays were written and, at
the same time, Fletcher lost his partner, Beaumont. In the case of *The Two Noble Kinsmen* and
Cardenio there is the external evidence of the
Stationers' Register entries, attributing both
to Shakespeare and Fletcher. *Cardenio* is lost
and *The Two Noble Kinsmen* internally exhibits
little to indicate that Shakespeare wrote any
part of it. Probably it was written by an en-
thralled imitator. Neither play was admitted
into the Shakespeare First Folio. None of the
evidence for Shakespeare's hand in *Sir Thomas
More* is conclusive, the paleographical argument being particularly weak because of the
extremely small sample of his authenticated
handwriting that is available for comparison
with Hand D. The sentiments in the 147 lines
in Hand D are not distinctive; in homily, play
and pamphlet they were a commonplace of Elizabethan thinking. The scene may well be
Shakespeare's along with the short speech on
greatness but the supposition has much wishful-
ness in it.

15 Everitt, E. B. *The Young Shakespeare. Anglis-
    tica* 2. Copenhagen: Rosenkilde and Bagger,
    1954. Pp. 73-9, 96-112.

    Compares details of style and the handling
of similar incidents in *Edward III* and *Edmund
Ironside* relying on patterns of imagery and in
part on Hart's vocabulary studies (item 5),
and concludes that the same author wrote both
of them in their entirety. Everitt contends
that the handwriting of Hand D in *Sir Thomas
More*, which he accepts as Shakespeare's, shows
signs of training in a legal hand. Tannenbaum's
attack on the identification, while alert and
vigorous, does not succeed. He prints tables
of likenesses and dissimilarities of four manuscripts: *Sir Thomas More*, *Edmund Ironside*,
Second Maiden's Tragedy and a letter in Dulwich
College. Everitt believes all four to be in
the hand of Shakespeare.

16   Greg, W. W. *The Shakespeare First Folio.*
         Oxford: At the Clarendon Press, 1955.
         Reprint. Oxford: Oxford University Press,
         1969, pp. 93-4, 98-9, 100, 102, 108, 118-20
         121-2, 126, 130-1, 134, 140, 167.

     Discusses *passim* and only briefly *Edward III,
Sir Thomas More, Cardenio* and *The Two Noble
Kinsmen* because they are excluded from the First
Folio. All four, with *Pericles*, are the substance of a long note (pp. 98-9). E. K. Chambers (item 2) considers the Countess of
Salisbury episode and one other scene to be by
Shakespeare, but Greg notes that uncertainty
about the date of the play and the company to
which it belonged hampers judgment. Most
students now accept the Shakespearean authorship
of the insurrection scene in *Sir Thomas More*
and of More's soliloquy. Objections by Tannenbaum and Schücking have not been well received,
while R. W. Chambers's latest version of his
essay on the Shakespearean ideas in *Sir Thomas
More* (item 105) and Bald's thoughtful judgment
(item 111) are as near proof as the nature of
the case allows. While Moseley's attribution
of *Cardenio* in his *Stationers' Register* entry
is not necessarily conclusive as to authorship,
Theobald's ascription in his *Double Falsehood*
is probably based on an early manuscript, perhaps bearing an attribution to Shakespeare.
The Two Noble Kinsmen was printed from prompt-
copy, was published as by Shakespeare and
Fletcher and is generally held to be the out-
come of a collaboration.

17   Law, Robert Adger. "Guessing about the Youthful
         Shakespeare," *Texas Studies in English,* 34
         (1955): 43-50.

     Review article of three recent books includ-
ing Everitt's *The Young Shakespeare* (item 15).
Everitt believes Shakespeare was a law clerk,
and learned to write with professional skill.
The handwriting of *Edmund Ironside* is in a professional hand which may have been Shakespeare's.
There are other manuscript plays in a similar
hand. Everitt accepts the identification of
Hand D in *Sir Thomas More* as Shakespeare's and

points out literary resemblances between *Edward
III* and Shakespeare's plays but they are slight.
Boswell, editor of the Malone Society reprint
of *Edmund Ironside*, determined that the manuscript is not autograph. Law concludes that it
cannot be attributed to Shakespeare.

18   Foakes, R. A., ed. *King Henry VIII. The Arden
        Shakespeare*. London: Methuen, 1957. Reprint
        with corrections and revisions, 1964.

     In the Introduction to this edition of *Henry
VIII* reference is made to the authorship questions, considered analogous, of *Cardenio* and
The Two Noble Kinsmen (pp. xix, xxiii). Foakes
accepts the collaboration of Shakespeare and
Fletcher in *Cardenio* and *The Two Noble Kinsmen*
without discussion.

19   Halliday, F. E. *The Cult of Shakespeare*.
        London: Duckworth, 1957. Pp. 16; 47-48.

     Determines that there is nothing to suggest
Shakespeare's hand in *Cardenio*, though it might
have been there before Theobald's improvements.
He most likely did have *Cardenio* manuscripts
and, finding the play was Fletcher's, altered it
to resemble Shakespeare. This would account for
the disappearance of the manuscript.
     Discusses Davenant's adaptation of *Two Noble
Kinsmen* (*The Rivals*) and concludes that the best
of Shakespeare's work has been eliminated and
all that remains is Fletcher's. Halliday notes
that in particular the invocations to Mars,
Venus and Diana were dropped.

20   Muir, Kenneth. *Shakespeare as Collaborator*.
        London: Methuen; New York: Barnes and Noble,
        1960. 164 pp.

     Reviews the arguments by Pollard, Greg,
Thompson, Wilson and Chambers in favor of
Shakespeare's authorship of the insurrection
scene and More's soliloquy in *Sir Thomas More*
(item 95) and accepts them as substantial if
not conclusive proof. Cites the contributions
of Spurgeon (item 98), Nosworthy (item 117)
and Shapiro (item 156) as providing additional

support. He believes Shakespeare took no part
in the planning of *Sir Thomas More* and accepts
a date of 1593.

On the basis of the imagery and image clusters that appear in *Edward III* and in Shakespeare's acknowledged plays Muir argues that
Shakespeare is the author of the Countess sequence (1.2 and Act 2), and the scene in which
the Black Prince refuses to surrender (4.4).
One image cluster (the *blot* cluster) not pointed
out by Armstrong (item 207) occurs in *Edward III*
and in *Love's Labor's Lost, Two Gentlemen of
Verona, Richard II, Venus and Adonis* and *The
Rape of Lucrece*. He cites characteristic Shakespearean images and numerous parallels between
Edward III and canonical plays, especially
Henry V and *Measure for Measure*, in support of
Shakespeare's authorship. An alternate theory
holds Shakespeare to be a hasty reviser of
Edward III, some scenes by the earlier poet being left comparatively untouched. Muir rejects
Brooke's (item 50) suggestion that Peele wrote
the play on the grounds that *Edward III* is unlike Peele in structure and diction. The form
and poetry are superior to almost all similar
plays except Shakespeare's canonical histories,
but not quite good enough to raise it above the
level of a chronicle play. There are links between the two parts but they are insufficient
to attain unity and the poetry in the non-Shakespearean part is subject to lapses into bombast.
The sense of situation in this part is not supported by a comparable power of characterization.
The sources are Froissart and Painter's *Palace
of Pleasure*.

Cardenio was acted at court at least twice,
once during the 1612-13 Christmas season and a
second time on 8 June 1613. It was entered in
the *Stationers' Register* on 9 September 1653 by
Humphrey Moseley as "A Play by Mr. Fletcher and
Shakespeare." Lewis Theobald, who knew nothing
of the records cited, presented a play in 1727
called *Double Falsehood*, which enjoyed considerable success and which he asserted was his
adaptation of a play by Shakespeare of which he
had three manuscript copies. *Double Falsehood*
is based on the Cardenio episode in Shelton's
translation of *Don Quixote* with the names of

the principals changed.   Theobald published it
in 1728.   No one ever saw his manuscripts and
his explanations of their origin are unsatisfactory; and yet the play seems to have identifiable traces of Fletcher and, less certainly,
of Shakespeare.   Theobald could not have known
of Moseley's attribution because he denied assertions by others that the play was reminiscent
of Fletcher.   It seems more likely that he had
a manuscript of some sort than that he composed
his adaptation in two different styles.   Further
conclusions are not possible.

On the basis of an extensive review of evidence adduced by other scholars on *The Two
Noble Kinsmen*--metrical and vocabulary tests,
parallels, multiple echoes, iterative imagery
and image clusters--and some first presented
here, particularly a newly identified image
cluster (*dirt*, *lust*, *crime*, *death*) Shakespeare
is the author of all of Act 1; 3.1 and 5.1, .3
and .4.   An analysis of the play itself clearly
reveals two hands, one that of a skillful crafts-
man of fashionable drama and a bona fide poet
but not of the highest order; the other the
maker of universal drama, neither facile nor
modish, and a poet of distinction whose verse
is sometimes dense and pregnant with meaning.
Fletcher deals, for example, in effective
theater and clever devices while Shakespeare
sets for himself the more challenging task of
character development.   That there are two playwrights is further attested to by inconsistencies in some important details and by the emphasis in certain scenes on the vagaries of
Fortune and the role of the gods in human affairs
which is virtually totally absent from the other
part.   Muir believes it reasonable that the play
was written in something of a hurry.   Shakespeare sketched out the play, wrote (broadly
speaking) the beginning and ending and left
Fletcher to complete it.   The source is the
Knight's Tale of Chaucer.

21   Bentley, Gerald Eades.   *Shakespeare: A Biograph-
     ical Handbook*.   New Haven: Yale University
     Press, 1961.   Pp. 130, 190-6.

     Discusses claims of authenticity of thirteen

plays ascribed to Shakespeare but not printed
in the Shakespeare First Folio including *Edward
III*, *Sir Thomas More*, *Cardenio* and *The Two Noble
Kinsmen*.   Bentley accepts the evidence for
Shakespearean authorship of parts of *Sir Thomas
More* and *The Two Noble Kinsmen*, considers it
possible that *Cardenio* was a Shakespeare-Fletch-
er collaboration, but notes approvingly that
Edward III is omitted from good modern editions.

22   Schoenbaum, S.   "Internal Evidence and the
     Attribution of Elizabethan Plays," *Bulletin
     of the New York Public Library*, 65 (1961):
     102-24.

     Reprint in somewhat abridged form in item
     29,   and in recast and considerably expanded
     form in item 31,   Section 3, "Avoiding Disas-
     ter," pp. 147-219.

23   Fogel, Ephim G.   "The Electronic Computer and
     Elizabethan Texts," *Studies in Bibliography*,
     15 (1962): 15-31.

     Brief allusion in passing to computer-assist-
     ed studies of attribution of *Edward III* (p. 26)
     and *Sir Thomas More* (p. 29).

24   Leech, Clifford.   *The John Fletcher Plays*.
     Cambridge, Mass.: Harvard University Press,
     1962.   Chap. 6, "Fletcher and Shakespeare,"
     pp. 144-68.

     Defines the reciprocal influences between
     Shakespeare and Fletcher and the evidence for
     collaboration between the two playwrights in
     three plays, *Henry VIII*, *The Two Noble Kinsmen*
     and *Cardenio*.   It is natural that Fletcher
     should be influenced by Shakespeare, but it is
     also possible that Shakespeare was to some de-
     gree influenced by his younger contemporary.
     Both kinds of influence can be discerned in
     The Two Noble Kinsmen.   Shakespeare was con-
     scious that simultaneous apprehension from two
     or more points of view was possible; Fletcher
     chose alternation rather than simultaneity of
     presentment.   These differences, which appear
     in *Two Noble Kinsmen*, provide evidence of dual

authorship. Leech discerns Shakespeare's hand
in the first and fifth acts but says that while
Shakespeare wrote part of the play, remembering
his own earlier work, the major impression is
that it is Fletcher's. He concurs in Gamaliel
Bradford's judgment that the first half of
Double Falsehood appears to contain Shakespearean passages while the denouement owes something
to *All's Well That Ends Well*, a reminiscence
which he believes points to Fletcher. *Cardenio*
was probably a collaboration to which Shakespeare made some contribution while the total
effect is characteristic of Fletcher's work.
Theobald undoubtedly made some use of a Jacobean original which was either identical with
or derivative from the play performed at court
and entered by Moseley on the *Stationers' Register*.

25   Jackson, MacD. P.   "Shakespeare and *Edmund Iron-
       side*," *Notes and Queries*, 208 (1963): 331-2.

     Discusses Everitt's use of image clusters
(item 15) in asserting Shakespeare's authorship
of *Edmund Ironside*, including the "*blot* cluster,"
not in Armstrong's pioneering study (item 207),
first identified by Muir (item 20) in *Edward
III*, and notes that Muir relies primarily on the
presence of peculiarly Shakespearean image clusters in *Edward III* and *The Two Noble Kinsmen*
as demonstrating his participation in those
plays. Jackson tests the integrity of the "*blot*
cluster" by tracing more than fifty occurrences
of the key-word in Spenser, Kyd and Marlowe and
found that in no case did more than a few com-
ponent elements of the Shakespearean cluster
occur within comparable distance of the key-
word. He also reports a disconcerting find of
Armstrong's "*beetle* cluster"--*beetle, crow,
other birds, mouse* or *bat, night, death, madness,
fairies, cliff*--in Shelley's poem *The Boat on
the Serchio*: *beetle, rooks, owl, lark, thrush,
swallow, bat, night, death, brains* for *madness,
brow of a hill*. He believes the validity of
image clusters as evidence for authorship is
diminished by this discovery.

26   Partridge, A. C. *Orthography in Shakespeare
      and Elizabethan Drama: A Study of Collo-
      quial Contractions, Elision, Prosody and
      Punctuation.* London: Arnold; and Lincoln:
      Nebraska University Press, 1964. Chap. 7,
      "The Manuscript Play *Sir Thomas More*: List
      of Contractions in dramatic use by 1600,"
      pp. 43-66. App. 4, "The Hands in *Sir Thomas
      More*," pp. 169-71. App. 7, "Shakespeare and
      The Two Noble Kinsmen," pp. 180-1.

      Analyzes the orthographical habits of Munday,
Heywood, Chettle, the scrivener, and Shakespeare, and the proposed dates of their contributions to *Sir Thomas More*, and concludes that
the original play was written "by Munday, Heywood (?) and Chettle" (p. 63) between 1593 and
1597 for the Admiral's Men who found it defi-
cient. Revisions were undertaken by Munday,
Heywood, Chettle and Dekker but still the play
was unsatisfactory and was disposed of to the
Lord Chamberlain's Men. Shakespeare added to
it by 1601 to fill out the conception of More
and his high sense of office, but when Tilney
demanded removal of objectionable parts, the
task of completing the play was abandoned. The
composite manuscript of *Sir Thomas More* is a
valuable document for the study of the orthography of Elizabethan dramatic authors. App. 4
summarizes the accepted division of the handwritings in *Sir Thomas More*.
      Partridge briefly sets forth some views
about *The Two Noble Kinsmen* based on his orthographic studies: the subject of the play was
probably Shakespeare's; the planning of the
play is unlike Shakespeare, the opening song is
his. The textual history of the play is complex: the Chamberlain's had an old *Palamon and
Arcite* that Shakespeare partially revised about
1611; then Beaumont and Fletcher, with Fletcher
doing most of the work, revised it further for
the production of 1613; it was finally retouched
by another, unknown writer between 1624 and 1626
for a revival in 1626 which is the version that
was printed in 1634.

27 Hobday, C. H.   "Why the Sweets Melted: A Study
      in Shakespeare's Imagery," *Shakespeare Quar-*
      terly, 16 (1965): 3-17.

      Traces a process of development of Shake-
speare's well known image clusters centered on
flattery, *dog*, *sweets* and *knee*. These occur in
association with a number of other images which
Hobday identifies as four different groups of
references within the same image cluster and
which are linked within each group and between
groups in ways not fundamentally logical. The
key ideas in the groups, in addition to *flat-*
tery, are: A--*dream*, *sleep*, *sweet* and *king* or
queen; B--*glass*, *face*, *hair*, *eyes* and *knee*; C--
sweet (or *candy* as a verb), *poison* or *venom*,
winter, *ice* or *hail*, *cold*, *melt* or *thaw*, *sun*,
brook or *stream*, *drop*, *tears* and *stone*; D--*dog*
(*spaniel* or *cur*), *fawning*, *sweet* or *candy*, *melt*,
and *knee* or *kneel*. Group A was the first to
crystallize and is found in both comic and tragic
associations (*Taming of the Shrew*, *Richard III*,
Romeo and Juliet and *Richard II*). Group B also
occurs early, in *Two Gentlemen of Verona* and,
notably, in the Countess scenes of *Edward III*.
Elements of Group A and almost all of the terms
of Group C are also found in those scenes.
Richard II, *Julius Caesar* and *As You Like It*
echo the forms of the cluster in *Edward III*.
The Two Noble Kinsmen contains several image-
clusters, most extensively in the first scene,
which includes Groups B and C, a parallel to
Group D, and a large number of words outside of
the clusters that Shakespeare associated with
flattery, which in itself is not mentioned but
the pleading of the three Queens and their
kneeling posture reminds the author of flattery.
There is also in the same scene a sequence of
images from Groups B and C which closely follows
a similar sequence in *Richard II*, both describing the effects of sorrow on the face but with
the images transformed in a personal way, and a
similar parallel sequence occurs between *The*
Two Noble Kinsmen and *Edward III*. This interrelated series of associations can only be explained by accepting the hypothesis of common
authorship between the canonical plays and parts
at least of *Edward III* and *The Two Noble Kinsmen*.

28   Campbell, Oscar James and Edward G. Quinn, eds.
      The Reader's Encyclopedia of Shakespeare.
      New York: Crowell, 1966. *Edward III*, p. 198;
      Sir Thomas More, pp. 799-800; *Cardenio*,
      p. 97; *The Two Noble Kinsmen*, pp. 914-8.
      Includes a facsimile of part of folio 9 of
      the manuscript of *Sir Thomas More*, p. 800,
      and a transcript of the portion reproduced,
      p. 979.

      Reviews scholarship and summarizes recent
      findings especially of authenticity studies of
      Edward III, Sir Thomas More and *Cardenio*. The
      treatment of *The Two Noble Kinsmen* is more com-
      prehensive including a discussion of the text,
      date and sources, a plot synopsis, comment, a
      stage history, a brief bibliography and selec-
      tions from critical discussions of the play.
      Campbell in his comment finds that the most
      profitable way of approaching the play is by
      way of Fletcher's romances rather than by way
      of Shakespeare's last plays. Seen from that
      point of view the play can be enjoyed as one of
      the best of Jacobean romantic tragedies. Shake-
      speare wrote 1.1, .2 and .3; 3.1; and all of
      Act 5 except scene 2.

29   Erdman, David V. and Ephim G. Fogel, eds. *Evi-
      dence for Authorship: Essays on Problems of
      Attribution.* Ithaca: Cornell University
      Press, 1966.

      Reprints with commentary by the editors a
      series of essays selected to provide a conspec-
      tus of methods and materials of attribution
      studies. Reprinted, in edited form, are items 22,
      111 and 227. An annotated bibliography of
      Elizabethan drama has a section on Shakespeare
      (pp. 432-94) which lists and describes papers
      other than those reprinted. There are sub-
      sections on *Edward III* (pp. 478-80), *Sir Thomas
      More* (pp. 480-82) and *The Two Noble Kinsmen*
      (pp. 486-94). In the course of an ample review
      of published papers on the *Henry VIII* author-
      ship controversy (pp. 457-78) the editors allude
      to *The Two Noble Kinsmen* on pp. 460-62, 465,
      467, 469, 471 and 476. In the review of *The
      Two Noble Kinsmen* authorship debate (pp. 486-90)

there is a brief discussion of *Cardenio* (pp.
486-7). Erdman and Fogel find that as regards
these two plays there is a "growing consensus"
among scholars to include *The Two Noble Kinsmen*
in the canon but that the evidence for *Cardenio*
as a Shakespeare-Fletcher collaboration is
"none too satisfactory" (p. 486).

30 Proudfoot, G. R.   "Shakespeare and the New
     Dramatists of the King's Men, 1606-1613,"
     Later Shakespeare, Stratford-upon-Avon
     Studies 8. Edited by John Russell Brown and
     Bernard Harris. London: Arnold, 1966, pp.
     235-61.

Assesses the relations during Shakespeare's
last decade in the theater between him and the
rising playwrights of the King's Men: Jonson,
Beaumont and Fletcher, Tourneur and Webster.
Since Jonson became increasingly active in
writing masques for the Court, the activities
of Beaumont and Fletcher became dominant which
leads to a discussion of the reciprocal influences between these new playwrights and Shakespeare.   There are three plays involved: *Cardenio*, *Henry VIII* and *The Two Noble Kinsmen*.
Since *Cardenio* survives, if at all, only in a
heavily adapted version by Theobald (*Double
Falsehood*) and because there is no external
evidence for collaboration in the composition
of *Henry VIII*, the principal discussion centers
on *Two Noble Kinsmen*.   The quarto title page
(1634) says that it was written by Fletcher and
Shakespeare but a close analysis of the structure of the play leads Proudfoot to suggest a
third hand.   He sees Shakespeare as the author
of the beginning (Act 1) and the ending (5.1,
.3 and .4).   In the center scenes Fletcher car-
ries the main plot forward, his assignment being to exploit the conflict between the love of
Palamon and Arcite for each other and their
competing love for Emilia.   The third element
comprises the subplot of the Jailer's Daughter
including the May-day morris dance in which she
takes a part.   This may be an interpolation and
possibly an afterthought.   Proudfoot cites dis-
locations at the transition between 2.1 and 2.2
and at 5.4.48 and, noting the findings of F. O.

Waller pointing to interpolation (item 272),
shows that if the subplot of the Jailer's Daughter and the morris dance are detached and some
twenty lines of 5.4 are deleted the play is coherent and complete except that Palamon's es-
cape from prison is not explained. These elements of the play exist separate from the main
plot and may have been the work of a third playwright. In explanation Proudfoot offers this
hypothesis based on a suggestion by Bertram
(item 233): following the burning of the Globe
on 29 June 1613 the King's Men, urgently in need
of a new play for the autumn at Blackfriars,
decided to press to an early conclusion a play
Shakespeare had already begun. Support for this
idea is seen in the prolog's reference to "our
losses" and in the epilog's promise of a better
play "ere long" which Bertram thinks is intended
as an explanation of the hasty composition of
The Two Noble Kinsmen. Proudfoot rejects Bertram's conclusion of Shakespeare's sole authorship and tentatively suggests that the King's
Men arranged to have Fletcher write the middle
acts while Shakespeare composed Act 5 and "a
third dramatist ... wrote the subplot scenes of
the Jailer's Daughter and the morris dance"
(p. 260), which were then presumably interpolated into the main body of the play. He does
not suggest who the "third dramatist" may have
been.

31   Schoenbaum, S. *Internal Evidence and Elizabeth-
         an Dramatic Authorship: An Essay in Literary
         History and Method*. Evanston: Northwestern
         University Press, 1966.

         Summarizes and assesses the authorship find-
ings of students of Elizabethan drama with particular emphasis on developments since the
founding of the New Shakespere Society (1873).
Schoenbaum notes neutrally Capell's advocacy of
Shakespeare's participation in *Edward III*, supported by Oliphant, Muir and Hart but opposed
by Robertson (pp. 20, 86, 125-7, 188).
         Shakespeare's hand is now universally recog-
nized to be present in *Sir Thomas More*. The
convergence of internal evidence--paleographic,

bibliographical, linguistic and critical--in
the symposium of Pollard et al., *Shakespeare's
Hand in the Play of Sir Thomas More*, leads to a
single destination, Shakespeare. The protesters,
Tannenbaum and Schücking, have not shaken the
thesis, while other scholars--Bald, Jenkins,
Alexander, Sisson, Spurgeon and Muir--have accorded support. Nosworthy (item 117) makes an
impressive case on evidence of language and
thought for Shakespeare's authorship of the
twenty-one lines of Addition III, More's soliloquy on greatness (pp. xix, 36, 86, 104-7, 124-5,
133-4, 166, 182, 224-5, 230).

With a measure of dubiety Schoenbaum cites
Oliphant's efforts to determine the participation of Shakespeare and Fletcher in *Cardenio* by
a study of *Double Falsehood* (pp. 123, 125).

He reviews the contributions of Spalding and
Hickson to the discussion of *The Two Noble Kinsmen* authorship question. Spalding's array of
internal evidence--verse, imagery, classical
allusions--is supported by Hickson's demonstration of the presence of two writers of dissimi-
lar and unequal powers, citing parallels in
style, structure and characterization to Shakespeare's acknowledged plays. In his studies of
the verse of *The Two Noble Kinsmen* he hinted at
the significance of double-endings and end-
stopped lines, leading to the well-known verse
tests. Littledale's edition (1876-85) of *The
Two Noble Kinsmen* includes the most thorough
study of authorship in the nineteenth century.
Littledale assigned to Shakespeare 1.1, .2, .3
and .4; 2.1; 3.1 and .2; 4.3; and 5.1, .3 and
.4, based on tests of rhyme, light and weak
endings, end-stopped lines and double endings,
and a scene-by-scene citation of parallels to
acknowledged plays. Hart's vocabulary studies
(item 5) and Mincoff's imagery studies (item
215) support the admission of *Two Noble Kinsmen*
to the canon. Bertram's case (item 233) for
Shakespeare as the sole author of *Two Noble
Kinsmen* has not won acceptance, nor has Ellis-
Fermor's denying his participation (item 226),
but Waller's bibliographic and linguistic evidence (item 272), supporting dual authorship,
has (pp. 4, 14, 16, 28-33, 51-6, 125-8, 136,
166, 179, 188, 225).

32   Clayton, Thomas.   "Internal Evidence and Eliza-
        bethan Dramatic Authorship: An Essay in
        Literary History and Method: Review Article."
        Shakespeare Studies, 4 (1968): 350-76.

        Reviews comprehensively Schoenbaum's *Internal
   Evidence and Elizabethan Dramatic Authorship*
   (item 31) including incidental discussions *passim* of possible Shakespearean participation in
   Sir Thomas More and *The Two Noble Kinsmen*.
   Clayton accepts the consensus for the authenticity of "the More fragment" (pp. 354-5) and
   inclines toward recognizing *The Two Noble Kinsmen* as a Fletcher-Shakespeare collaboration
   (pp. 353, 355).

33   Harbage, Alfred, gen. ed.   "The Canon," *The
        Complete Pelican Shakespeare*.   Baltimore:
        Penguin, 1969, pp. 18-20.

        On the basis of style and analogy with his
   acknowledged work it has been asserted that
   Shakespeare wrote the Countess episode in *Edward III*.   On orthographic and stylistic grounds
   it has been cogently argued that he supplied
   the mob scenes in *Sir Thomas More*.   Lost manuscript plays include *Cardenio* but the attribution of authorship is likely to be as fic-
   titious as for the rest of the apocrypha.
   There is a strong probability that Shakespeare
   played some part in the composition of *Two Noble
   Kinsmen*.

34   Schoenbaum, S.   *Shakespeare's Lives*.   Oxford:
        Clarendon Press, 1970.   Pp. 60-1, 488.

        There is no conclusive proof of Shakespeare's
   participation in *Edward III* (p. 488).   Although
   three pages of *Sir Thomas More* may be in Shakespeare's hand, the play was excluded from the
   Shakespeare First Folio.   *Cardenio*, attributed
   to Shakespeare and Fletcher by Moseley, is lost,
   or does it survive in *Double Falsehood*?   The
   first quarto of *Two Noble Kinsmen* ascribes the
   play to Shakespeare and Fletcher, but it too
   was omitted from the Shakespeare First Folio.
   Heminges and Condell overlooked or deliberately
   rejected these plays (pp. 60-1).

35 Kermode, Frank. *Shakespeare, Spenser, Donne: Renaissance Essays*. London: Routledge, 1971. Chap. 10, "The Final Plays," pp. 219-59.

Treats *Pericles*, *Cymbeline*, *Winter's Tale* and *Tempest* as a group having common themes; *The Two Noble Kinsmen*, which is predominantly Fletcher's play, is handled separately. *Henry VIII* is more profitably treated with the other chronicle plays. Suggests that the stimulus to Shakespeare's interest in dramatic romance may have been the great narrative romances, Sidney's *Arcadia* and Spenser's *Faerie Queene*. It is not improbable that Shakespeare collaborated with Fletcher in *The Two Noble Kinsmen*. The external evidence of the attributions of both *Cardenio* and *Two Noble Kinsmen* to the two of them is not lightly to be disregarded. Fletcher's dominance in *The Two Noble Kinsmen* is demonstrated by the fondness for spectacular effects, the peculiar nastiness in the handling of the subplot of the Jailer's Daughter and in the salacious banter between Palamon and Arcite, the flippant prolog and epilog and, in general, the unShakespearean over-extension of the possibilities and lack of natural dynamism. It is difficult to believe that Shakespeare planned the play. While he may have written a great deal of it, Shakespeare had nothing to do with the plot. The Shakespearean parts of *The Two Noble Kinsmen* fall below our expectations which may have been because of failing powers, or simply because of a lack of interest in the play.

36 Barnet, Sylvan, gen. ed. "The Shakespeare Canon," *The Complete Signet Classic Shakespeare*. New York: Harcourt Brace Jovanovich, 1972. P. 5.

Some experts believe that three pages of the manuscript *Sir Thomas More* are in Shakespeare's handwriting but the attribution is not widely accepted. *The Two Noble Kinsmen* has increasingly gained acceptance as having been written at least in part by Shakespeare.

37   Bradbrook, M. C.   "Shakespeare and his Collabo-
          rators," *Proceedings of the World Shakespeare
          Conference, Vancouver, August 1971*.   Edited
          by Clifford Leech and J. M. R. Margeson.
          Toronto: Toronto University Press, 1972.
          Pp. 21-36.

          Reprint in substance in item 43, Chap. 13.

38   Wentersdorf, Karl P.   "Imagery as a Criterion
          of Authenticity: A Reconsideration of the
          Problem," *Shakespeare Quarterly*, 23 (1972):
          231-59.

          Brief comment on authenticity questions of
          Edward III, Sir Thomas More and *The Two Noble
          Kinsmen* in the course of this comprehensive
          discussion of imagery and especially image clus-
          ters in Shakespeare's plays.   With some relative-
          ly minor reservations Wentersdorf accepts the
          evidence for Shakespeare's presence in these
          three plays.

39   Muir, Kenneth.   "A Trick of Style and Some Im-
          plications," *Shakespeare Studies*, 6 (1973):
          305-10.

          Finds internal rhyme of varying kinds common
          in *Hamlet, Othello, Macbeth, Timon of Athens,
          Antony and Cleopatra, Cymbeline, Winter's Tale*
          and *Tempest*, and points out that the number of
          such rhymes rises steeply in plays of the final
          period.   The device is also used by Beaumont
          and Fletcher in *Philaster*, but at a lower rate
          than in *Cymbeline* and since Shakespeare employed
          internal rhyme as early as *Hamlet* probably Flet-
          cher is following Shakespeare.   Examples occur
          more frequently in those parts of *Henry VIII*
          and *The Two Noble Kinsmen* traditionally assigned
          to Shakespeare as compared to the allegedly
          Fletcherian scenes.   Several examples also occur
          in *Double Falsehood*.   Muir presents his findings
          as "tentative" and notes that *Coriolanus* has
          comparatively few internal rhymes.

40   Proudfoot, G. R.   "*The Two Noble Kinsmen* and the
          Aprocryphal Plays," *Shakespeare: Select*

Bibliographical Guides.   Edited by Stanley
Wells.   London: Oxford University Press,
1973.   Pp. 389-97.

Claims that the possibility of Shakespeare's
hand in plays outside the First Folio receives
support from the near exclusion of *Troilus*
which left room for *Timon* which otherwise might
have been omitted.   In the second issue of the
Third Folio seven plays were attributed to him
but only *Pericles* has been accepted.   The internal evidence for *Edward III* is strong and
various, linked to Shakespeare's early histories and the sonnets in vocabulary, imagery,
structure and theme.   Convincing arguments have
been advanced for Shakespeare's authorship of
two parts of *Sir Thomas More* (Additions IIc and
III) in Greg's edition of 1911 and the symposium
of 1923 (item 95).   The other attributions to
Shakespeare are of two plays of the latest
years of his career.   *Cardenio* used the episode
of Cardenio and Lucinda from Shelton's translation of *Don Quixote* (1612).   Theobald published a play he claimed was an adapted version
of *Cardenio*, entitled *Double Falsehood*.   He
denied Fletcher's participation.   *Double Falsehood*'s association with the Shakespearean play
has been challenged but Freehafer (item 194)
has demonstrated the possibility that Theobald
could have had one or more Jacobean manuscripts.
The case for Shakespeare's participation in
The Two Noble Kinsmen was strongly established
by Littledale's parallels of thought and expression between *Two Noble Kinsmen* and Shakespeare's accepted plays, and subsequently supported by Hart's vocabulary studies (item 5).
Critics such as Spencer (item 202) and Edwards
(item 230) have tried to explain the divided
nature of *The Two Noble Kinsmen* which may be
traceable to collaboration or to a Shakespearean view of love that is radically different
from his earlier plays and as disturbing as
that of *Troilus* after *Twelfth Night*.

41   Ruoff, James E.   *Handbook of Elizabethan and
      Stuart Literature*.   New York: Crowell, 1975.
      "The Book of *Sir Thomas More*," pp. 393-4;
      "*The Two Noble Kinsmen*," pp. 440-1.

Describes the manuscript of *Sir Thomas More*, and discusses the arguments for and against Shakespeare's authorship of Addition IIc and for and against the various dates of composition suggested by scholars. Ruoff finds all evidence bearing on both questions purely internal and "shaky" (p. 394). He accepts Waterson's ascription of *The Two Noble Kinsmen* to Shakespeare and Fletcher and notes the traditional division of the play between the two dramatists. A summary of the plot is given followed by a brief criticism in which Ruoff finds that the "romance bears all of the marks of Fletcher's high-blown tragicomedies" (p. 440), and implies that he planned the play.

42   Schoenbaum, S. *William Shakespeare: A Documentary Life*. New York: Oxford University Press in association with The Scolar Press, 1975. Pp. 157-60, 228, 257. 2d ed., rev. *William Shakespeare: A Compact Documentary Life*. New York: Oxford University Press, 1977. Pp. 214-19, 279, 314.

Describes the manuscript of *Sir Thomas More* and traces scholarly opinion regarding the authenticity of Addition IIc, concluding that a broad spectrum of evidence supports the attribution to Shakespeare. Schoenbaum briefly discusses the problem of dating the manuscript and leans toward 1600-01. He accepts a Fletcher-Shakespeare collaboration in *The Two Noble Kinsmen*. A photographic facsimile of Folio 9 recto of the *Sir Thomas More* manuscript containing the conclusion of More's speech to the mob is included.

43   Bradbrook, M. C. *The Living Monument: Shakespeare and the Theatre of his Time*. Cambridge University Press, 1976. Chap. 13, "Shakespeare as Collaborator," pp. 227-41.

Considers the authorship of the Shakespearean portions of *Sir Thomas More* well established. The play is of the jest-book style of history: a great man at one with the common people. It appeals to the solidarity and sense of humanity of the Londoners. In More's plea to the rebels

the living Shakespearean accents of persuasion,
urgent and passionate, are heard.

Since neither author nor company is given on
the title-page of *Edward III*, it could hardly
have been a notable success. Comparison of the
Countess scenes with Edward IV's wooing of Lady
Grey (*3 Henry VI*, 3.2) shows the former to be
set and rhetorical, and therefore unShakespearean, while the latter is lively. The presence
of lines from the sonnets is an argument against
Shakespeare's participation since he does not
repeat himself literally. The apparent con-
nections of *Edward III* to *Henry V* and *Measure
for Measure*, not yet written when *Edward III*
was published, are actually of a non-dramatic
rhetorical persuasion and do not establish common authorship. The literary references tie
the date of composition close to the date of
publication (1595). If Shakespeare had acted
in it in his early years he may have remembered
some of it when writing later plays as he had
Rare Triumphs of Love and Fortune and *Sir Clyamon and Sir Clamydes* in his mind when writing
Cymbeline.

Jacobean audiences would have hastened to
see *The Two Noble Kinsmen* for the scenes of the
Jailer's mad daughter and the morris-dance.
The play was perhaps commissioned to provide a
setting for the antimasque borrowed from Beaumont's court *Masque of the Inner Temple and
Gray's Inn*. War and love constitute the argument of the play given by spectacle rather than
debate. The imagery is appropriate to this
play and is unquestionably Shakespearean. The
flatness of the characters allows the handling
of a situation with both heterosexual and homo-
sexual elements. The masque-like concern with
roles rather than characters allows the topic
of homosexuality (Palamon-Arcite; Theseus-Piri-
thous; Emilia-Flavina) to become pervasive
without being acknowledged. The stately grief
of the main story is contrasted with the subplot which in itself is a kind of self-parody.
If acted briskly and with variety the two halves
of the play might cohere as theatrical collage.
It is difficult to resist the claims of the
title-page of the 1634 Quarto of *The Two Noble
Kinsmen* for the collaboration. The case for

Shakespeare's part-authorship is strong. The
reasons for the collaboration were speed (to
take advantage of the notable success of Beaumont's antimasque), variety and the commercial
advantage of two famous playwrights' names on
the playbill. Shakespeare wrote the opening
and closing acts while Fletcher wrote the middle,
remembering his partner's past successes. The
main design was Fletcher's and hardly amounted
to a drama which explains why it was omitted
from the Shakespeare First Folio.

44   Zesmer, David M. *Guide to Shakespeare*. New
         York: Barnes & Noble, 1976. "Postscript:
         The Two Noble Kinsmen," pp. 452-4.

Finds that although some critics reject
Shakespeare's authorship of *The Two Noble Kinsmen* because of alleged weakness in characterization and lack of sustained intellectual and
emotional force, there is no compelling reason
to question the external evidence of the *Stationers' Register* entry and the Quarto title-
page ascribing the play to Shakespeare and
Fletcher. The consensus assigns to Shakespeare:
1; 3.1 and .2; 5.1, .3 and .4. The use of Beaumont's antimasque in *The Two Noble Kinsmen* and
the allusion in Jonson's *Bartholomew Fair* set
the date in 1613. The source is Chaucer's
Knight's Tale; the subplot of the Jailer's
Daughter is consistent with the philosophy of
the tale. The major theme of the play is the
destructive power of sexual love. Shakespeare
may have had a hand in *Edward III*, probably contributed to *Sir Thomas More*, and may have collaborated on *Cardenio*.

45   Leech, Clifford. "Masking and Unmasking in the
         Last Plays," *Shakespeare's Romances Recon-
         sidered*. Edited by Carol McGinnis Kay and
         Henry E. Jacobs. Lincoln and London: Uni-
         versity of Nebraska Press, 1978, pp. 40-59.

Demonstrates that masques-within-plays became fairly frequent in Jacobean drama but these
are not true masques in that they do not follow
the regular masque pattern; they are of neces-
sity too brief and generally adopt an ironic

twist. Not infrequently they are in reality
truncated masques or antimasques. The dance
presented by the schoolmaster in *The Two Noble
Kinsmen* is an adaptation of the second anti-
masque from Beaumont's *Masque of the Inner Temple and Gray's Inn.* In *Two Noble Kinsmen* it
has a distinctive quality in that it is basic-
ally comic but is tinged with sadness because
of the participation of the love-sick and de-
ranged Jailer's Daughter. Leech notes that we
have no evidence in *Double Falsehood* of a masque
in *Cardenio* but this is no assurance that the
play did not have one. He believes that Shakespeare and Fletcher worked together on *Two Noble
Kinsmen* and *Cardenio* and possibly on *Henry VIII.*

46 Muir, Kenneth. *Shakespeare's Comic Sequence.*
    Liverpool: Liverpool University Press, 1979.
    Chap. 6: *The Merchant of Venice*, pp. 55-6;
    and chap. 18: *The Two Noble Kinsmen*, pp. 192-
    202.

    Accepts the 1634 quarto title-page ascription
of *The Two Noble Kinsmen* to Shakespeare and
Fletcher. The first act is well planned and
well written. Although the characterization
tends to be conventional and somewhat flat, the
writing is clearly Shakespearean and shows no
signs of deterioration. He sets forth three
themes: friendship in its various modes, the
power of Fortune and the inscrutable workings
of the gods. The thirteen central scenes are
clearly Fletcher's and are inferior. The under-
plot of the Jailer's Daughter is bungled. Palamon and Arcite are less heroic and become merely elegant, sentimental figures. There is a
sudden drop in the quality of the poetry in the
prison scenes. The beginning of Act 3 and the
whole of the fifth act, except the second scene
and the first eighteen lines of the first scene,
exhibit the surge and thunder of Shakespeare's
final style. The invocations to Mars, Venus
and Diana are as vigorous as ever but Palamon's
prayer unexpectedly emphasizes the destructive
powers of the goddess of love. The gods answer
their votaries' pleas but not in the way they
expect. The stage directions in this scene are
elaborate and spectacular and are probably

Shakespeare's own. The plot of the play does
not allow for much subtlety nor depth of characterization, but the Blackfriars audience
probably preferred it that way. We are left
with mixed impressions: a sense of mystery,
the impossibility of understanding the workings
of providence and a gratitude for life.

Muir cites the humanity of Addition IIc of
Sir Thomas More as evidence of Shakespeare's
tolerance towards aliens and freedom from anti-
semitism.

47   Schoenbaum, S. *William Shakespeare: Records
        and Images.* New York: Oxford University
        Press, 1981. Pp. 47, 98-9, 109-13. Facsim-
        iles 52, 53, 54 (pp. 113-5); 148, 155, 156
        (pp. 226, 230).

Discusses the paleographic considerations
bearing on the question of the authorship of
the 147 lines in *Sir Thomas More* with emphasis
on the scholarly discussion since the publication of his documentary life of Shakespeare
(item 42) as the main part of a section entitled
"Shakespeare's Handwriting" (pp. 93-115).
Schoenbaum notes that recent comment has tended
to be cautionary, the side of the discussion
towards which he leans. He reviews the contributions of Huber, Hays and Ramsey (items 123,
139 and 141) on the negative and cites Sisson
(item 123) as balancing their views. He finds
a slight slip in Dawson's brief but ingenious
orthographical study (item 185) [which does not
materially affect Dawson's argument]. The kinds
of evidence supporting Shakespeare's authorship
of Addition IIc--paleographic, literary and
textual (especially *scilens*) are encouragingly
varied and the arguments are powerful, yet the
ascription remains a theory not a fact because
of the absence of external evidence. Reproduces
in photographic facsimile folios 8a, 8b and 9a
of **the manuscript** of *Sir Thomas More* and the
Stationers' Register entries of *Cardenio* and
The Two Noble Kinsmen.

DATES

See items 2, 7, 9, 20, 26, 28, 29, 42, 43, 44, 50, 53.

SOURCES

48   Hosley, Richard. *Shakespeare's Holinshed*.   New
       York: Putnam, 1968.

       Considers *Edward III* and *Sir Thomas More* as
     part of the sequence of historical plays of
     various authorship influenced by Holinshed,
     which deal with all but one (Henry III) of the
     fourteen rulers of England from John in 1199 to
     Henry VIII in 1509 (p. xviii).

49   Muir, Kenneth. *The Sources of Shakespeare's
       Plays*.   London: Methuen; and New Haven:
       Yale University Press, 1978.

       Suggests in a brief comment (p. 265) and a
     note (p. 310 n. 16) that, since Shakespeare and
     Fletcher collaborated on *Cardenio* and *The Two
     Noble Kinsmen*, perhaps they saw each other's
     work (on the model of Auden and Eliot) when
     they were writing *Cymbeline* and *Philaster*.
     Muir refers in passing to *Edward III* (p. 111)
     and to *Sir Thomas More* (p. 283) but in his
     Introduction says that "the apocryphal plays ...
     have been excluded from consideration" (p. 13).

TEXT AND EDITIONS

50 Brooke, C. F. Tucker, ed. *The Shakespeare
    Apocrypha*. Oxford: At the Clarendon Press,
    1908. Reprint. Oxford: At the University
    Press, 1967.

    Prints fourteen plays that Brooke considers
    entitled, on grounds of reason or custom, to a
    place among the doubtfully Shakespearean plays
    including *Edward III*, *Sir Thomas More* and *The
    Two Noble Kinsmen*. The text of *Edward III* is
    based on that of Warnke and Proescholdt; of
    Sir Thomas More on Dyce's edition; and of *Two
    Noble Kinsmen* on Littledale's edition. Refer-
    ence in the cases of *Edward III* and *Two Noble
    Kinsmen* is made to the quarto texts; and in the
    case of *Sir Thomas More* to the manuscript.
    Brooke also includes an appendix on *Sir Thomas
    More* in which he prints the earlier text of the
    revised passages.
        Considers *Edward III* in some ways the most
    extraordinary of the doubtful plays in the
    quality of its poetry and of the general excel-
    lence of the Countess episode. But the mawkish-
    ness of the dialog between Warwick and the
    Countess and the cloying sweetness of other pas-
    sages demonstrate that those parts of the play
    sometimes assigned to Shakespeare are certainly
    not his. Brooke suggests that Peele is the
    author even though he concedes it is finer than
    anything in Peele's acknowledged work. The
    sources are Holinshed and Painter, perhaps
    Froissart.

Credits Shakespeare with parts of two scenes
in *Sir Thomas More*: 1-172 of the insurrection
scene, and 1-21, 48-121, 241-282 **of the scene**
at More's house in Chelsea, the greatness soliloquy and the Faulkner sequence. Recognizes
the high poetic attainment of the insurrection
scene, its functional utility and its Shakespearean mode of thought. The other scene shares
the same general characteristics. If Shakespeare was ever concerned with any of the apocryphal plays, it was with this. The date of the
play, based largely on the mention of a Strange's
actor by name, is 1590-5. The main source is
Hall's Chronicle with three incidents taken
from Foxe's *Book of Martyrs*.

Metrical tests applied to *The Two Noble
Kinsmen* clearly indicate the presence of two
hands in the composition. One is undoubtedly
Fletcher. The incidence of double endings and
run-on lines in the part not by Fletcher approaches that in *The Winter's Tale* and *The Tempest* and coincides with the un-Fletcherian part
of *Henry VIII*. The undeniably Shakespearean
tone of the style is offset by the characterization which is not like Shakespeare. The
part of the play that is obviously not Fletcher's
contains some of the most brilliant Jacobean
poetry but lacks the psychological insight and
the philosophy of life worthy of the mature
Shakespeare. Brooke accepts Littledale's division of the play between the collaborators.
The structural and psychological imperfections,
the unnecessary coarseness of language and the
feeble imitation of Shakespeare eliminate him
as Fletcher's collaborator and advance Massinger's
candidacy, who for once may have risen to the
lofty poetry of *The Two Noble Kinsmen*. The
source is Chaucer's *Knight's Tale*.

Links *Cardenio* to *Double Falsehood* but dismisses it as having been assigned to Shakespeare
perhaps fraudulently by Theobald.

51   Greg, W. W. *The Editorial Problem in Shakespeare:
     a Survey of the Foundations of the Text*.
     Oxford: At the Clarendon Press, 1942. 3rd
     ed., rev. Oxford: Oxford University Press,
     1954.

Discusses in a note on *Pericles* the absence of *Pericles*, *Cardenio* and *The Two Noble Kinsmen* from the First Folio, as contrasted to the inclusion of *Henry VIII*. One possible explanation is that either *Henry VIII* is wholly Shakespeare's and the others are not; or *Henry VIII* is partly Shakespeare's and he had no hand in the others. Possibly Heminges and Condell did not intend to include in their collection plays that were not substantially Shakespeare's.

Greg cites *Sir Thomas More passim* in chap. 2, "Theatrical Manuscripts," noting Tilney's comments, the manuscript's value as an example of foul papers and of dramatic collaboration, its evidence about the relationship of an authorial manuscript to the prompt-book and concerning the division of theatrical manuscripts into acts and scenes.

52 Farjeon, Herbert, ed. *The Complete Works of William Shakespeare*. London: Nonesuch; and New York: Random House, 1953. 4 vols. Vol. 3 contains *The Two Noble Kinsmen, Edward III* and *Sir Thomas More*.

The text of *Edward III* is an old spelling diplomatic reprint of the British Library copy of the first quarto (1596) with notes of variant readings from the second quarto (1599).

The text of *Sir Thomas More* is a transcription based primarily on Greg's edition (1911) with some readings supplied from Dyce's (1844). The arrangement is a conflation of the original text with the additions inserted in place of the original passages which are given in the notes.

The text of *The Two Noble Kinsmen* is an old spelling diplomatic reprint of the Garrick copy of the quarto (1634) in the British Library.

The notes to all three plays, other than supplying the original readings in *Sir Thomas More* replaced by the additions, are minimal and chiefly textual.

53 Jewkes, Wilfred T. *Act Division in Elizabethan and Jacobean Plays 1583-1616*. Hamden, Conn.: Shoe String, 1958.

Edward III is undivided. The text is full with little evidence of adaptation. Stage directions are meager, frequently vague and appear to be largely authorial but there are several in the imperative mood. There is little evidence of the playhouse so an author's manuscript is indicated, though the copy may have been tentatively prepared for the stage. The probable date is before 1595 (pp. 231-2).

Sir Thomas More is briefly noted as completely undivided and dated c. 1593 (p. 9).

The Two Noble Kinsmen was printed from copy which came unmistakably from the playhouse. Imperative stage directions, anticipatory entrances, references to actors and properties definitely point to playhouse copy, probably a prompt-book. Date is 1613 (pp. 314-5).

54   Spevack, Marvin. *A Complete and Systematic Concordance to the Works of Shakespeare.* 6 vols. Hildesheim: Olms, 1968-70. Reprint (except for forty-three most frequent words). *The Harvard Concordance to Shakespeare.* Cambridge, Mass.: Harvard University Press, Belknap Press, 1973.

Includes *The Two Noble Kinsmen* and Additions IIc and III of *Sir Thomas More* based on the *Riverside Shakespeare* text.

55   Evans, G. Blakemore. "Shakespeare's Text: Approaches and Problems," *A New Companion to Shakespeare Studies.* Edited by Kenneth Muir and S. Schoenbaum. Cambridge: At the University Press, 1971. Pp. 222-38; 273-5.

Defines the extant materials for an examination of Shakespeare's text as *Venus and Adonis* and *The Rape of Lucrece* and thirty-nine plays, the thirty-six of the First Folio plus *Pericles*, *Sir Thomas More* and *The Two Noble Kinsmen*. Of these *Sir Thomas More* is of special interest since Shakespeare's holograph manuscripts underlie the printed texts of a number of the plays as we have them, perhaps as many as sixteen or seventeen, and the 147 lines of *Sir Thomas More* are now thought to be in Shakespeare's own hand. Some critics consider *Edward III* to be at least

in part Shakespeare's and in addition to the
extant plays there are the lost *Cardenio* and
Love's Labor's Won. Includes a facsimile of
fifteen lines of the *Sir Thomas More* manuscript.

56   Evans, G. Blakemore, textual ed. "Shake-
        speare's Text," *The Riverside Shakespeare*.
        Boston: Houghton Mifflin, 1976. Pp. 27-8,
        31.

        Although a number of critics have identified
Shakespeare's hand in parts of *Edward III* (particularly the Countess scenes) the play is not
included in this edition. The two passages
from the manuscript play *Sir Thomas More*, which
are now widely accepted as by Shakespeare, are
included. *Cardenio* is known only in a drastic
revision by Theobald whose manuscripts have
disappeared. Moseley's attribution is of uncertain authority. *The Two Noble Kinsmen* was
attributed to Shakespeare on the title-page of
the only quarto (1634) and has been admitted to
the canon.

57   Proudfoot, G. R., ed. *The Shakespeare Apoc-
        rypha*. 3 vols. Oxford: At the Clarendon
        Press, forthcoming.

        Planned to consist of fifteen plays: new
editions of the fourteen plays of the Tucker
Brooke edition (item 50), which includes *Edward
III*, *Sir Thomas More* and *The Two Noble Kinsmen*;
the fifteenth play will be Theobald's *Double
Falsehood*.

II
The Reign of King Edward III

II. *THE REIGN OF KING EDWARD III*

See the items in the section on The Plays as a Group, most of which comment on *Edward III*. Those that *do not* are items 1, 8, 11, 14, 18, 19, 24, 26, 30, 32, 35, 36, 39, 41, 42, 45, 46, 47, 54.

CRITICISM AND COMMENTARY

58   Golding, S. R. "The Authorship of *Edward III*," *Notes and Queries*, 154 (1929): 313-5.

Cites thirty parallels between *Edward III* and plays that Golding thinks were written by Robert Wilson, such as *The Cobbler's Prophecy, Three Lords and Three Ladies of London* and, most importantly, *A Larum for London*, and concludes that the author of *Edward III* was Wilson. If Wilson was capable of writing *Edward III* then his authorship of the three pages in *Sir Thomas More* need not cause any alarm (see item 97).

59   Osterberg, V. "The 'Countess Scenes' of *Edward III*," *Shakespeare Jahrbuch*, 65 (1929): 49-91.

Compares linguistic and verbal qualities of Shakespeare's acknowledged work with *Edward III* and concludes that there is significant common ground not only in verbal correspondences but also in affinities of thought. Metrical analysis under headings such as versification, pause and double endings speaks positively for Shakespeare's authorship. In its theme of love and lust and its metrical and stylistic peculiarities, the play fits into the group of his writings of the time (1592-4) and presents the characteristics of Shakespeare's methods at that time. The Countess episode is poetically equal to Shakespeare's undoubted work. Osterberg closely evaluates Robertson's suggestion that Greene wrote *Edward III* and concludes that Greene could not have anticipated so much that is in Shakespeare's later plays nor would Shakespeare have over the years imitated Greene's original ideas. Before 1592 there existed a play on Edward III written probably by Marlowe, Kyd and Greene. The Chamberlain's Men acquired it about the time the theatres reopened in 1594. Shakespeare already had a plan to use the story of the Countess of Salisbury as a companion piece to *Lucrece*. He rewrote the Countess scenes of the existing play, preserving odd bits reminiscent of Kyd and Greene and hints from other sources including Greene's *James IV* and Painter's Novel 46 (on the Countess episode). Shakespeare spent some half hour touching 1.1; 3; 4 and 5 in a cursory manner leaving traces of his pen. The Countess scenes are indisputably Shakespearean and the balance of evidence is decidedly in favor of Shakespeare's authorship.

60   Lindabury, Richard J. *A Study of Patriotism in the Elizabethan Drama*. Princeton: Princeton University Press, 1931.

      Notes that in the Salisbury-Villiers episode *Edward III*, unlike other early history plays, portrays the French as honorable. *Edward III* is cited *passim* in regard to various general topics (e.g., fear of invasion, reputation of foreigners).

61   Crundell, H. W. "Drayton and *Edward III*," *Notes and Queries*, 176 (1939): 258-60, 356-7.

      Contends that the general likeness of *Edward III* to Drayton's poem *The Battaile of Agincourt*, the specific incident in both the poem and the play of the flight of crows (or ravens) and its effect on the French troops, and the similarity of the diction of the Countess scenes to Drayton's *England's Heroical Epistles* make it more reasonable to regard *Edward III* as an early work of Drayton's than to ascribe the play to Shakespeare or Greene. "Its best scenes are lyrical declamation rather than dialogue and there was no greater master of this kind than Michael Drayton" (p. 259). In response to a portion of Tillotson's argument (item 62) against Drayton--the date of *Edward III*--Crundell asserts without citing his evidence that Drayton "was in touch with Chettle and Munday in 1596" (p. 356).

62 Tillotson, Kathleen. "Drayton and *Edward III*," *Notes and Queries*, 176 (1939): 318-9.

Disputes Crundell's assignment of *Edward III* to Drayton (item 61) on the grounds that in Drayton's *Heroical Epistles* the wooer of the Countess of Salisbury is the Black Prince, not Edward III; that the parallels between the play and Drayton's poems do not prove more than that Drayton knew the anonymous play. The parallel of the flight of crows shows Drayton "recalling the play, since none of the chronicles mentions such omens" (p. 319). The date of *Edward III* (before December 1595) is against Drayton's authorship because there is no evidence of his having written for the stage at that early date.

63 Wells, William. "Thomas Kyd and the Chronicle-History," *Notes and Queries*, 178 (1940): 218-24; 238-43.

Notes that Sarrazin assigned *Edward III* to Kyd and that Robertson believes that Kyd shared in a four- or five-fold collaboration that wrote the play. Sykes's claims for Peele, following Brooke, as the author of *Edward III* cannot be allowed because Peele's known work is more loosely constructed and handles historical facts much more freely. Wells believes *Edward III* to be entirely Kyd's on the basis of parallels of structure and vocabulary with the

anonymous *Troublesome Reign of King John* which
it is his purpose in this essay to prove was the
work of Kyd. The two-part *Henry IV* obviously
owes something to the influence of *Edward III*.

64   Reese, Gertrude C. "The Question of the Suc-
        cession in Elizabethan Drama," *Texas Studies
        in English*, 22 (1942): 59-85.

     Brief discussion in passing of succession
theme in *Edward III*.

65   O'Connor, Frank. *The Road to Stratford*.
        London: Methuen, 1948. Pp. 24-32; 44-7.

     Concludes that *Edward III* is entirely Shake-
speare's based on the affinities to *Lucrece* and
the Sonnets and comparable examples of antithe-
sis in *Edward III* and in *Richard II, King John,
Julius Caesar* and *Measure for Measure*. Dates
the play at the end of 1593 or the spring of
1594. Its anti-Scottish sentiments account for
its exclusion from the First Folio.

66   Bradbrook, M. C. *Shakespeare and Elizabethan
        Poetry*. London: Chatto and Windus, 1951.
        Pp. 208-11.

     Compares the structure of *Henry V* to the
"pseudo-Shakespearean" *Edward III* (p. 209).
The unity of theme in *Edward III* has a close
similarity to *Henry V* in spite of the fact that
the earlier play is divided into two parts.
The fight against odds in *Edward III* in the
double battle of Crecy-Poitiers corresponds to
Harfleur-Agincourt in *Henry V*. The descrip-
tions of the two invading fleets in the two
plays (*Edward III* 3.1 64-78 and *Henry V*,
second chorus 5-17) contain close parallels.
In both plays the odds favor the French who
taunt the English and urge them to surrender.
Audley's speech about death foreshadows Henry's
contempt of death before Agincourt. Shakespeare may have had the earlier play in mind
when he wrote *Henry V*.

67 Bethell, S. L.   "The Comic Element in Shake-
        speare's Histories." *Anglia*, 71 (1952-3):
        82-101.

        Notes lack of comic element in *Edward III*,
    "an unusually good ... early play" (p. 85).

68 Muir, Kenneth.   "A Reconsideration of *Edward
        III*," *Shakespeare Survey*, 6 (1953): 39-48.

        Reprint in revised form in item 20, chap. 2.

69 Dobson, Willis B.   *Edward the Third: A Study
        of its Composition in Relation to its
        Sources.*   University of Texas diss., 1956.
        Abstract: *Shakespeare Newsletter*, 7 (1957):
        19.

        Finds Countess scenes superior to rest of
    Edward III in style and other respects and con-
    cludes they are an interpolation that echo
    Shakespeare's style but are not necessarily his.

70 Baldwin, T. W.   *On the Literary Genetics of
        Shakspere's Plays 1592-1594.*   Urbana: Uni-
        versity of Illinois Press, 1959.   Pp. 232-7.

        Assigns *Edward III* to the Admiral's on the
    basis of the structure of the *dramatis personae*.
    The prevailing Admiral's pattern comprises a
    principal male character of the Tamburlaine
    type (King Edward).   The second line is usually
    an opponent of the male lead (King John); the
    third male part is an oratorical dignitary
    (Warwick); and the fourth a young warrior
    (Prince Edward).   There is usually one major
    woman's part (Countess of Salisbury) and a
    second less prominent character (Philippa).
    The only deviation from this pattern in *Edward
    III* is the position of the Black Prince who by
    a narrow margin (nine lines) is the second most
    important part.   Baldwin explains this as de-
    manded by the heroic tradition and concludes
    that *Edward III* conforms to the formula of
    Admiral's plays of about 1589.

71 Wentersdorf, Karl P. "The Authorship of *Edward
     III*," *Dissertations Abstracts International*.
     21/04 (1960): 905A. Ann Arbor: University
     Microfilms International, 1960.

         Compares images, iterative imagery and image
     clusters in *Edward III* with those in acknowledged
     Shakespearean plays (principally *3 Henry VI*,
     Richard II and *Henry V* but frequently including
     other plays, *Venus and Adonis* and *Lucrece*); and,
     for contrast, with those in *The Spanish Tragedy*
     and the poetry of Sir Thomas Wyatt. The imagery
     of *Edward III* substantially corresponds to
     Shakespeare's. Examines some key stylistic
     features such as techniques of characterization,
     versification, vocabulary and dramatic structure
     and finds that the characterization is not un-
     like Shakespeare's; that verse tests are incon-
     clusive; that applying Hart's (item 5) vocabu-
     lary tests demonstrates that the characteris-
     tics of the vocabulary of *Edward III* agree with
     Shakespeare's; and that the method of exposition
     of *Edward III*, its use of mirror-scenes and of
     dramatic irony have affinities with the canon-
     ical plays. The strongest argument for identi-
     fying the author of *Edward III* as Shakespeare
     is the correspondence of image clusters with
     those recognized by Spurgeon as peculiarly
     Shakespearean. Cites mention in *Edward III* of
     English ship Nonpareil that fought against the
     Spanish Armada, the anachronistic reference to
     naval artillery at the battle of Sluys and the
     Stationers' Register entry of *Edward III* of 1
     December 1595 as establishing 1588-1595 as the
     early and late limits of date of composition.
     Comparison of imagery statistics with the Shake-
     spearean plays divided into four periods as-
     sociates *Edward III* with the early plays, es-
     pecially the early histories, and *Lucrece*. Tests
     of feminine endings, run-on lines, split lines
     and pausation indicate that *Edward III* may have
     preceded the Yorkist tetralogy. The sum of the
     evidence indicates an early date, probably about
     1589-91. See item 86.

72 Reese, M. M. *The Cease of Majesty: A Study of
     Shakespeare's History Plays*. London: Arnold,
     1961. Pp. 85-8.

Concurs in Tillyard's identification of the central theme of *Edward III* as the education of princes (item 13). Notes Edward is self-disciplined in his wooing of the Countess and in the siege of Calais, and possesses positive virtues--courage, leadership, patriotism, decisiveness. The reflective qualities of *Edward III* place it above the chronicle plays and establish it as an early example of a Shakespearean type history play. Printed in 1596, the play was probably written three or four years earlier. Shakespeare has sometimes been regarded as the author, at least of the Countess scenes.

73 Lambrechts, G. "*Edward III*, Oeuvre de Thomas Kyd," *Etudes Anglaises*, 16 (1963): 160-74.

Argues on the basis of parallel passages, limited to verbal and some of only a few words, between *Edward III* and *The Spanish Tragedy*, *Soliman and Perseda* and occasionally *Cornelia*, supported by an analysis of style under headings such as Phonetique, Syntaxe, Vocabulaire and L'orthographe that *Edward III* is entirely the work of Thomas Kyd. Dates the play between 9 May 1594 because of the allusion to *Lucrece* and 30 December 1594 when Kyd was dead.

74 Talbert, Ernest William. *Elizabethan Drama and Shakespeare's Early Plays: An Essay in Historical Criticism*. Chapel Hill: University of North Carolina Press, 1963. Pp. 91-3; 110-13; 168-9.

Contends that there are two chief structural movements in *Edward III* flowing from current strains of thought. The first is the concept that personal wantonness alone may become malfeasance and tyranny. This is seen in Edward's agreeing to kill both the Countess's husband and his Queen, but the danger is averted by the Countess's staunch virtue, and the King goes on to demonstrate his heroic qualities. The second structural movement informs the last three acts which exhibit a concern for glory and honor as well as a defiance of Fortune, fear, and death exhibited both by King Edward and the Black Prince.

75   Howarth, R. G.   *A Pot of Gillyflowers: Studies
        and Notes*.   Cape Town: by the author, 1964.
        Mimeographed.

        Argues that *Edward III*, in its blend of ma-
     terial drawn from the English chronicles and
     Italian romance, resembles generally Greene's
     Scottish Historie of James IV.   The story is the
     same--royal adulterous pursuit of a high-born
     lady leading to shame and repentance.   As the
     theme and treatment, the style and verse resem-
     ble Greene's it may perhaps be accepted as his.

76   Koskenniemi, Inna.   "Themes and Imagery in
        Edward III," *Neuphilologische Mitteilungen*,
        65 (1964): 446-80.

        Reviews assessment of imagery by Muir (item
     20), and concurs in his judgments.   There are
     some differences of emphasis not noted by Muir,
     and Koskenniemi cites some new image patterns
     (e.g., from writing, printing, engraving and
     books in general).   The character of the itera-
     tive imagery, its presence in all parts of the
     play and the fact that the main groups of images
     cluster around the central themes point to a
     single author.   A comparison of the images in
     Edward III with those in Peele's *Arraignment of
     Paris*, *The Battle of Alcazar*, *Edward I* and
     David and Bethsabe reveals Peele's frequent use
     of classical images not present in significant
     numbers in *Edward III*.   The love episodes in
     Edward III and *David and Bethsabe* are handled
     entirely differently; and while *Edward III* has
     many compound epithets, Peele's plays do not
     make much use of them.   These differences sug-
     gest that Peele did not have a hand in *Edward
     III*.   The effort by Lambrechts (item 73) to
     assert Kyd's authorship of *Edward III* fails be-
     cause many of the images and parallels he cites
     are commonplace.   The few striking parallels in
     imagery and diction are best accounted for by
     assuming the author of *Edward III* knew Kyd's
     Spanish Tragedy and *Soliman and Perseda*.   The
     large number of correspondences in *Edward III*
     of imagery, diction and theme with those found
     by scholars in Shakespeare's canonical plays
     establishes Shakespeare as a candidate for iden-

tification as the author, and the allusion in
Edward III to *Lucrece* (Brooke, item 50, 2.2.
194-7) appears to be in the tone of the author
of the poem. The weight of the internal evidence seems to indicate that Shakespeare wrote
part of *Edward III* or that he revised the whole.

77   Jackson, MacD. P.   "*Edward III*, Shakespeare, and
        Pembroke's Men," *Notes and Queries*, 210
        (1965): 329-31.

     Demonstrates that the actors who constructed
from memory the texts of the bad quartos of
2 Henry VI and *3 Henry VI* recalled passages from
Edward III as well as some from other early
plays that belonged to Pembroke's Men. The bad
quarto of *2 Henry VI* was published as *The First
Part of the Contention betwixt the two famous
Houses of York and Lancaster* in 1594; and that
of *3 Henry VI* (*The True Tragedy of Richard Duke
of York*) in 1595. It is generally accepted
that these and several other memorially recon-
structed plays belonging to Pembroke's were
assembled by the players upon the collapse of
the company in the summer of 1593. (See A. S.
Cairncross. "Pembroke's Men and Some Shakespearian Pirates." *Shakespeare Quarterly*, 11
[1960]: 335-49.) From the evidence presented
by Jackson it is established that the date of
composition of *Edward III* must be not later
than 1592 and perhaps earlier; and that the
company that owned the play was Pembroke's with
whom it is thought by some scholars that Shakespeare was associated at that time. Jackson
points out that one of the recollections in *The
True Tragedy* is from a Countess scene (2.1)
which disposes of the hypothesis that the Countess episode is a late interpolation, thus supporting Wentersdorf's contention (item 71) that
the entire play is by Shakespeare.

78   Ribner, Irving.   *The English History Play in the
        Age of Shakespeare*. 2d ed., rev. London:
        Methuen, 1965. Reprint. New York: Octagon,
        1979. Pp. 142-50.

     Accepts Tillyard's theory (item 13) that the
theme of *Edward III* is the education of princes.

Scholars have taken different positions on the
authorship from all Shakespeare's to finding
nothing of Shakespeare in it. Ribner inclines
to accept Hart's (item 5) and Muir's (item 20)
conclusions that the Countess scenes are Shakespearean. The dramatic intensity of these
scenes, their didactic character and political
content, and the general excellence of the poetry clearly point to Shakespeare as the author
of the Countess scenes "and probably a good
deal more of the play is" his work (p. 143).
The sources of the play are Holinshed, Froissart and Painter. The historical material is
freely telescoped in time to present a portrait
of a victorious national hero. The central political problem of the play is the relation between the King's law and moral law as seen in
the Countess sequence, the Villiers-Salisbury
incident and its sequel in the conflict between
Prince Charles and his father, King John of
France, regarding the safe conduct for Salisbury.
Edward III is a highly philosophical play in
which the didactic and moral functions of history
are clearly exemplified.

79 Hoy, Cyrus. "Renaissance and Restoration Dramatic Plotting," *Renaissance Drama*, 9 (1966):
247-64.

Compares the plotting of the Countess sequence
of *Edward III* to that of comparable sequences
in Jacobean and Caroline plays (*A King and No
King*, *The Malcontent*, *Revenger's Tragedy*) and
concludes that the *Edward III* plot is admirably
effective and at the same time simple and direct.
Unlike the later plays the plot of *Edward III*
foregoes exploiting the potentially sensational
and highly suggestive features of the Countess
episode. The scene in which the Countess proposes that the King kill her husband and his
Queen has potential for romantic not to say
erotic sensationalism of the kind that Jacobean
dramatists found irresistable but which is entirely unexploited in *Edward III*. The treatment
of the situation is completely straightforward,
consisting in a plain depiction of a clash of
purposes and setting forth in bold, clear strokes

the responses of the opposing wills, unlike
oblique Jacobean treatments of similar situ-
ations.   These differences point to the larger
transformations of form and spirit which dramatic style was to undergo in the transition
from Renaissance to Baroque.

80   Freeman, Arthur. *Thomas Kyd: Facts and Prob-
        lems*. Oxford: at the Clarendon Press, 1967.
        P. 180.

     Finds Lambrechts's arguments (item 73) for
Kyd's authorship of *Edward III* nonsensical.
The parallels he cites do not support his con-
tention.

81   Bevington, David.   *Tudor Drama and Politics: A
        Critical Approach to Topical Meaning*. Cam-
        bridge, Mass.: Harvard University Press,
        1968. Pp. 202-4.

     King Edward's claim to the French throne in
Edward III is valid and provides an ethical
foundation justifying the war against the usur-
per King John. Edward spares the peasantry and
France's orchards, vineyards and children and
even the burghers of Calais. The author of
Edward III, whether Shakespeare or another, was
clearly of Shakespeare's persuasion about the
morality of warfare.

82   Grivelet, Michel. "Shakespeare's 'War with
        Time': The Sonnets and *Richard II*," *Shake-
        speare Survey*, 23 (1970): 69-78.

     Cites parallels between *Richard II* (2.4.18-21;
3.2.36-53) and Sonnet 7 concerning kingly majesty, Phoebus, the sun and fire which also occur
in *Edward III* (Brooke, item 50, 2.1.143-8, 298-
402) and finds the conclusion inescapable that
the writer of the passages in *Edward III* had in
mind the images in *Richard II* and Sonnet 7.
Grivelet traces the origin of both images to
Book II of Ovid's *Metamorphoses*.

83   Muir, Kenneth. "Shakespeare's Poets," *Shake-
        speare Survey*, 23 (1970): 91-100. Reprint
        in revised form in *Shakespeare the Profes-*

sional and Related Studies. London: Heine-
mann; and Totowa, N. J.: Rowman and Little-
field, 1973. Chap. 2, "Shakespeare's Poets,"
pp. 22-40.

Finds Shakespeare's attitude towards poets
rarely serious or complimentary. Usually he
views them with irony, satire or contempt. One
exception is Lodowick, a poet who appears in
the second act of *Edward III* which Muir believes
was written by Shakespeare. Edward seeks to
advance his suit to the Countess of Salisbury
by means of a poem. Lodowick, who earlier
speaks of the King's infatuation in terms which
express his admiration for the Countess and his
low opinion of Edward's advances, is commanded
to compose the poem. The King gives him detailed instructions without telling him to whom
the poem is to be addressed and Lodowick com-
poses a line and a half, in one phrase calling
the lady chaste and in a succeeding phrase comparing her to Judith, to both of which Edward
emphatically objects. Lodowick undoubtedly was
attempting to remind the King that he was contemplating committing a sin. He is the only one
of Shakespeare's poets whose action is credit-
able.

84 Riggs, David. *Shakespeare's Heroical Histories:
     Henry VI and its Literary Tradition*. Cam-
     bridge, Mass.: Harvard University Press, 1971.
     Pp. 17, 27, 60, 73, 80-3.

Describes *Edward III* as a full scale portrait
of a legitimate king claiming his French birth-
right. The play centers on Edward, his weakness
and desire for the Countess and his heroic qualities. *Edward III* is a coherent play that attempts to project a version of heroic honor
based on feudal custom and medieval chivalry,
dedicated to the glory of God, the service of
the poor and fatherless and England's peace.
Nevertheless there are elements of aggression
and conquest and Edward's chivalry is purely a
matter of personal dignity. While the order of
composition is not settled, *1 Henry VI* is the
artistic sequel to *Edward III*, dated 1590.

85 Lewis, John S. "The Rash Oath in *Edward III*," *Allegorica*, 1 (1976): 269-77.

Accepts the two recognized unifying themes of *Edward III* as the education of the prince and the mirror of kingship but points out that the prevalence of rash oaths throughout the play also is a unifying influence. Edward extracts oaths from both the Countess and her father, Warwick; and when the Countess finally convinces the King that she will preserve her chastity she forces him to swear never again to press his attentions on her. This tri-partite pattern of oaths is reminiscent of the casket scene in *The Merchant of Venice*. In the military scenes the Earl of Salisbury frees a French captive Villiers to obtain for him (Salisbury) a pass to go through French territory to Calais upon his oath to return after getting the pass. Charles, Duke of Normandy, tries to persuade Villiers not to return but he insists and the Duke signs the pass. Salisbury is later captured and the French King would have him executed but is dissuaded by his son because he had signed the pass thus giving his word that Salisbury had free passage. These types of oaths are not so unusual, examples occurring in *Captain Thomas Stukeley* and *2 Fair Maid of the West*.

DATE

86 Wentersdorf, Karl P. "The Date of *Edward III*,"
   Shakespeare Quarterly, 16 (1965): 227-31.

   Argues that the generally accepted date of
   1594-5 for the composition of *Edward III* is
   late. The vivid description of the great de-
   struction wrought by naval artillery and the
   mention of the exploits of the English ship
   Nonpareil are allusions to the battle in the
   English Channel which resulted in the defeat of
   the Spanish Armada, anachronistically included
   in *Edward III* as part of a report of the naval
   battle of Sluys. *Edward III* was therefore
   written between the end of 1588 and 1 December
   1595 when it was entered in the *Stationers'
   Register*. There is no other external evidence
   yielding a more precise date than 1588-1595 but
   the nationalistic tone of *Edward III* and its
   affinities in diction, imagery and treatment of
   subject matter to *1 Henry VI* indicate a date
   about 1589-90.

See also items 2, 7, 43, 50, 53, 59, 61, 62, 65,
   67, 70, 71, 72, 73, 77, 84, 87, 89, 91.

SOURCES

See items 2, 20, 50, 59, 61, 62, 75, 78, 82, 90, 91.

TEXT AND EDITIONS

87 Farmer, John S., ed. *The Reign of King Edward
      III*. Tudor Facsimile Texts No. 78. Edin-
      burgh and London: by the Editor, 1910.
      Reprint. New York: AMS, 1970.

      Photographic facsimile of the British Library
      copy of the first quarto (1596). Farmer notes
      in his introduction that "from internal evidence
      it is clearly shown that the play was written
      early in 1589." He does not cite the evidence.

88 Crawford, Charles. *The Marlowe Concordance*.
      Louvain: Uystpruyst, 7 pts., 1911-32. Re-
      print. New York: Franklin, 1964; Kraus,
      1967.

      Includes concordance to *Edward III* because
      "there is such an extraordinary and general
      agreement between the vocabulary used in this
      play and certain scenes of the *First Part of
      Henry VI*" (p. vii), which Crawford believes may
      be in part Marlowe's. Based on the text of
      G. C. Moore Smith, 1897.

89 Winny, James, ed. *Three Elizabethan Plays*.
      London: Chatto and Windus, 1959. Contains
      Edward III, *Midas* and *Mucedorus*.

      The *Edward III* text is based on the first
      quarto (1596) with doubtful and corrupt pas-
      sages emended to provide a version for school
      use.

The play falls into two distinct halves with
the Countess episode and the military scenes
having little in common. Thus *Edward III* lacks
unity of action, but is a good representative
of the tradition which Shakespeare brought to
maturity. The diction of *Edward III* is not
that of the established Shakespeare but there
is dramatic power of a kind of which only Marlowe and Shakespeare were capable in 1594. It
cannot be entirely Shakespeare's work because
two different hands are clearly discernible,
the one greatly superior to the other. Parallels with *Two Gentlemen of Verona* and *Measure
for Measure* suggest Shakespeare as the poet of
the first part of *Edward III*. The play was
popular since it was played sundry times about
the City of London and was reprinted in 1599.

90   Armstrong, R. L., ed. *Edward III*. *Anglistica*
        14, *Six Early Plays Related to the Shake-
        speare Canon*. Edited by E. B. Everitt and
        R. L. Armstrong. Copenhagen: Rosenkilde and
        Bagger, 1965. Pp. 195-247.

The text of *Edward III* is based on the first
quarto (1596) collated with the second quarto
(1599), and has been modernized. Significant
textual variants are noted.
   Armstrong discusses sources in the introduction, agreeing with R. M. Smith (*Froissart
and the English Chronicle Play*, New York: 1915)
that the play is based on Froissart who treats
of almost all of the material in the play. For
the Countess episode, the play also draws on
Painter's *Palace of Pleasure*, Novel 46, which
has a more dramatic account derived from Ban-
dello. There are two minor incidents taken
from Holinshed which are not in Froissart; the
Countess's gibing at the Scots from her battle-
ments, and the English archers, having shot
their arrows, resort to hurling flints at the
French. There are three specific bits in *Edward
III* not in any known source: the otherwise unknown ships Nonpareil and Black Snake (whose
names are suspiciously secular) in the French
fleet at Sluys [but see items 71 and 86]; the
symbol of the pelican on the Black Prince's ar-
mor; and a French commander, Chatillion, other-

wise unknown, who is in charge of a major division of the French forces.

91   Armstrong, William A., ed. *The Reign of King
      Edward the Third*. *Elizabethan History Plays*.
      The World's Classics, No. 606. London:
      Oxford University Press, 1965.

      Modern text based on that of G. C. Moore
Smith (1897) with reference to the quartos of
1596 and 1599. Holinshed's *Chronicle* and Painter are the sources. The theme of the play is
the education of princes and in that respect
parallels Shakespeare's trilogy on Prince Hal.

92   Jackson, MacD. P. "A Note on the Text of *Edward
      III*," *Notes and Queries*, 216 (1971): 453-4.

      Suggests solutions to two textual cruxes in
Edward III at 4.4.44 and 4.4.142 (Brooke, item
50). The first is traceable to an authorial
tangle, pointing to foul papers as copy text;
the second is compositorial error. In a foot-
note the editor, J. C. Maxwell, proposes a
metrical correction at 4.7.35.

93   Kozlenko, William, ed. *Disputed Plays of
      William Shakespeare*. New York: Hawthorn,
      1974.

      Reproduces photographically the text and
notes of eleven of fifteen apocryphal plays
from the 1860 edition of *The Doubtful Plays of
Shakspere*, edited by Henry Tyrrell. Includes
Edward III.
      Kozlenko's introduction is limited to a sum-
mary of earlier opinion regarding the authorship
of *Edward III* and to an attempt by means of
parallel passages to establish Shakespeare's
presence in the play. He concludes that the
text is the result of a hasty revision by Shakespeare of a play by another dramatist, certain
scenes (unspecified) having been entirely rewritten, others left largely unchanged.

94   Lapidus, Fred, ed. *The Raigne of King Edward
      the Third*. New York: Garland, 1980.

A critical, old-spelling edition based upon the first quarto (1596) collated with the second quarto (1599) and eight earlier editions: Capell (1760), Tyrrell (1851), Delius (1854), Collier (1878), Warnke and Proescholdt (1886), Smith (1897), Brooke (1908, item 50) and Armstrong (1965, item 90).

After examining authorship studies by Hart (item 5), O'Connor (item 65) and Wentersdorf (item 71), Lapidus determines that while the evidence adduced is not conclusive, it is very probable that Shakespeare wrote the whole of *Edward III*. He accepts Wentersdorf's date of about 1590, and R. L. Armstrong's distribution of the sources (item 90). The printer of the first quarto was Thomas Scarlet and his copy was authorial foul papers. The quartos are described and earlier editions briefly evaluated.

III
Sir Thomas More

III. *SIR THOMAS MORE*

See the items in the section on The Plays
as a Group, most of which comment on *Sir
Thomas More*. Those that *do not* are items
1, 5, 8, 11, 18, 19, 24, 25, 27, 30, 35,
39, 45.

CRITICISM AND COMMENTARY

95 Pollard, A. W., ed. *Shakespeare's Hand in the
Play of Sir Thomas More*. Cambridge: At the
University Press, 1923. Reprint. Cambridge:
Cambridge University Press Library Edition,
1967. A. W. Pollard, Preface and Introduc-
tion. W. W. Greg, "The Handwritings of the
Manuscript." Sir E. Maunde Thompson, "The
Handwriting of the Three Pages Attributed to
Shakespeare Compared with his Signatures."
J. Dover Wilson, "Bibliographical Links be-
tween the Three Pages and the Good Quartos."
R. W. Chambers, "The Expression of Ideas--
Particularly Political Ideas--in the Three
Pages and in Shakespeare." W. W. Greg, ed.,
"Ill May Day. Scenes from the Play of Sir
Thomas More." W. W. Greg, ed., "Special
Transcript of the Three Pages." 243 pp.

Pollard in the Preface sets forth the object
of the book: to strengthen the evidence of the
existence of three pages written by Shakespeare
in his own hand as part of the play of *Sir
Thomas More*. In the Introduction Pollard traces
the scholarship of *Sir Thomas More* to 1923 and
provides an assessment of the findings of the
other contributors to the symposium. He dis-

cusses the significance of the mentions of the
player Goodale and the theatrical wig maker
Ogle in relation to the date of composition and
decides that the probable date of original composition is late in 1593 or early in 1594 and
that the revisions were completed before the
prentice uprising in the late spring and early
summer of 1595. In an Appendix to the Introduction Pollard prints accounts of the anti-
alien disturbances of 1595, 1586 and 1593 from
contemporary documents.

In "The Handwritings of the Manuscript" Greg
describes the various hands and identifies hands
S (Munday), E (Dekker) and C (playhouse scribe).
He evaluates the evidence as to the date and
concludes that the play was written sometime between 1593-4 and 1597.

Thompson describes and analyzes the extant
Shakespearean signatures and finds that they
provide scant but sufficient evidence for purposes of identification. He analyzes the handwriting of Addition IIc (which he incorrectly
calls Addition D) first in general, then letter
by letter, including abbreviations. He concludes
that the resemblances, especially of certain
characteristic forms of letters such as the
spurred *a* and the elongated needle eye associated with the letters *w* and *m*, and, to a lesser
degree, with other letters, are sufficient to
identify the writer of the Addition with the
writer of the Shakespearean signatures.

Wilson compares punctuation, spellings and
misprints in the good Shakespearean quartos
with the handwriting of the three pages and
finds that the copy of the good quartos was very
much like that of the three pages of *Sir Thomas
More*. He sums up: Shakespeare like the writer
of Addition IIc used the English hand; they both
preferred the capital *C* to the lower case letter;
that Shakespeare's plays exhibit the same slips
in letter formation as those found in the three
pages; that the author of the Addition and Shakespeare were both old-fashioned spellers and
shared the extremely rare spelling *straing* and
the apparently unique spelling *scilens*. Bibliography can find nothing un-Shakespearean in the
Addition. In an Appendix Wilson lists a large

number of spellings found in the three pages
with parallels from the Shakespearean quartos.
    R. W. Chambers discusses political ideas in
the three pages and in Shakespeare. He developed and elaborated his ideas, originally set
forth here, in later versions of this essay.
See item 105.
    Greg prints "a consecutive and more or less
readable text of the insurrection scenes"
(p. 191) and transcribes anew the three pages
of Addition IIc with a few changes from his
Malone Society text of 1911.

96 Greg, W. W. "Shakespeare's Hand Once More."
        Times Literary Supplement, 24 November 1927,
        p. 871 and 1 December 1927, p. 908. Re-
        print. *W. W. Greg: Collected Papers*, edited
        by J. C. Maxwell, Oxford: At the Clarendon
        Press, 1966, pp. 192-200. In a note to the
        reprint (p. 192 n. 1) Greg says he is pre-
        senting this article "in the form origin-
        ally intended as a considered summing up of
        the purely palaeographical evidence in favor
        of" identifying Hand D as Shakespeare's.

        Reviews the palaeographic case adduced by
Sir Edward Maunde Thompson (item 95) establish-
ing Shakespeare as the author of Addition IIc
of *The Booke of Sir Thomas Moore* and observes
that while Thompson's general conclusion is no
doubt valid some of the findings regarding
specific letter formations are, upon more searching examination of the documents, not entirely
convincing. Nevertheless if part of Thompson's
case fails, the remaining part that stands is
sufficient palaeographically for purposes of
identification. Greg concludes:
        "(1) The palaeographical case for the hands
of [the Shakespeare signatures] and D being the
same is stronger than any that can be made out
for their being different.
        (2) The hand of [the signatures] is more
nearly paralleled in D than in any other dramatic document known to us.
        (3) Setting [the signatures] aside, it can
be shown that D was not written by any dramatist of whose hand we have adequate knowledge.

(4) On purely palaeographical grounds there
is less reason to suppose that all six signatures were written by the same hand than there
is, granting this identity, to suppose that the
hand of the signatures also wrote the addition
to *More*."

97 Golding, S. R. "Robert Wilson and *Sir Thomas
    More*," *Notes and Queries*, 154 (1928): 237-9;
    259-62.

Cites thirty parallels between *A Larum for
London* and Wilson's "accredited plays" (p. 238)
such as *Fair Em, Sir John Oldcastle, The Pedlar's
Prophecy* and *A Knack to Know a Knave* establish-
ing Wilson's authorship of *A Larum*. Comparison
of the whole of *Sir Thomas More* with Wilson's
plays (including *A Larum*) shows frequent uses
in both of the same words and phrases such as
plague on, plodding, true as the gospel and *a
god on earth*. In *Sir Thomas More* and *A Larum*
the image of the waters overbearing their banks
occurs. There are also parallels of ideas such
as the general prejudice against strangers,
their presence driving up prices and rents, the
gluttonous habits of aliens and the danger of
reducing English workmen to beggary, as expressed by the rebels in *Sir Thomas More* and the
Artificer in *The Pedlar's Prophecy*. These sentiments are characteristic of Wilson who attacked
foreigners and was well-known as a chauvinist.
If Shakespeare revised the insurrection scene,
he did it with Wilson's draft in front of him.
Golding says that the paleographic question is
for experts but he is of the opinion that there
is a close resemblance between Wilson's handwriting and Hand D.

98 Spurgeon, Caroline F. E. "Imagery in the *Sir
    Thomas More* Fragment," *Review of English
    Studies*, 6:23 (1930): 257-70.

Proposes to add to the studies of style,
handwriting, spelling and ideas of Addition IIc
of *Sir Thomas More* a detailed study and comparison of the imagery in the fragment to the
known work of Shakespeare. In the 147 lines

there are twelve images which fall into familiar Shakespearean categories. Seven of the
twelve express an idea or an image that recurs
many times in Shakespeare and parallels of the
other five are to be found in the canonical
plays. Each of the images in the 147 lines of
Sir Thomas More is taken up in turn and specific identifications with Shakespearean images
are made. They fall under the usual Shakespearean headings, are found in the usual pro-
portions and are paralleled in the known plays.
The greater number of them express ideas and
applications of ideas peculiarly characteristic
of Shakespeare, are repeatedly found in his
work and are expressed in language reminiscent
of Shakespeare. The cumulative evidence they
offer forms one more link in the gradually
strengthening chain of proof leading to the belief that the fragment was written by Shakespeare.

99 Bald, R. C. "Addition III of *Sir Thomas More*,"
     Review of English Studies, 7 (1931): 67-9.

     Considers that the internal evidence is of
itself sufficient to assign Addition III of *Sir
Thomas More* to Shakespeare. The soliloquy of
twenty-one lines contains verbal parallels,
echoes and in a few cases the same phrases from
Othello, *Macbeth*, *Troilus*, *Richard II*, *Hamlet*,
Henry V, *2 Henry IV* and *Taming of the Shrew*.
In characteristic Shakespearean fashion the
parallels while close are parallels of thought,
not direct quotations, but all have a genuine
Shakespearean ring.

100 Greg, W. W. *Dramatic Documents from the Eliz-
      abethan Playhouses: Stage Plots, Actor's
      Parts, Prompt Books*. Vol. 1: Reproductions
      and Transcripts. Vol. 2: Commentary. Oxford:
      At the Clarendon Press, 1931. Reprint.
      Oxford: Oxford University Press, 1969.

     Contains a photographic facsimile of the
title on the wrapper of *Sir Thomas More* and of a
portion of sc. 8, fol. 12a (beginning of
Faulkner sequence) in Hand C (1: Nos. 2A and 2B).

The manuscript is the original fair copy in
Munday's hand, altered and augmented in five
other hands. Although the name of an actor,
Thomas Goodale, appears, it is unlikely the
play was ever acted. The date is disputed but
Greg inclines to 1593, indicating that it be-
longed to the amalgamation of Strange's and the
Admiral's in that year (2: 224-5).

101 Law, Robert Adger. "Is Heywood's Hand in *Sir
       Thomas More?*" *Texas Studies in English*, 11
       (1931): 24-31.

       Summarizes Tannenbaum's arguments in favor
of identifying Hand B as that of Heywood. *The
Captives* and *The Escapes of Jupiter* are autograph
manuscripts of Heywood's. Resemblances of B's
writing to the Heywood manuscripts are not evident. B prefers simple vowels to doubled and
usually to diphthongs, *ow* to *ou*, medial *s* to
medial *c*, and *y* to *i*, while Heywood does not.
Law finds nothing in the orthography or style
to suggest that Heywood is B. The handwriting
while somewhat similar does not furnish convincing evidence. The case is not proved.

102 Jenkins, Harold. *The Life and Work of Henry
       Chettle*. London: Sidgwick & Jackson, 1934.
       Pp. 59-71.

       Describes and evaluates the contribution of
Chettle (whom he accepts as the author of Hand A)
to *Sir Thomas More*. Jenkins reviews the state
of the scholarship of the play to the date of
the book, generally agreeing with the findings
of the symposium (item 95) and with the later
work of Spurgeon (item 98). He concludes that
Chettle's seventy-one lines in *Sir Thomas More*
are superior to the portion of the play that
they replace. He anticipates Shapiro (item 156)
in assigning a date of 1590 to Munday's *John a
Kent and John a Cumber*, dating *Sir Thomas More*
about 1593 and the additions in the following
year. Chettle made a small contribution to
John of Bordeaux which was a Strange's play.
He could also have participated in *Sir Thomas
More* which belonged to the same company, especially since he was known to be friendly with

Munday in 1592.

103 Chambers, R. W. *Thomas More.* London: Cape; and
      New York: Harcourt, Brace, 1935. Pp. 43-7;
      150-1; 278. Reprint. Ann Arbor: University
      of Michigan Press, 1958.

   Asserts the opinion that the Elizabethan
play of *Sir Thomas More*, despite its inconsistencies and confusions, is important because it
accurately depicts More's continuing popularity
with the London populace in spite of the efforts
of the anti-More propagandists of the sixteenth
and seventeenth centuries. Foxe's tales of
cruelty and Hall's sneers at More did not affect
London opinion which remembered him as a friend
to the city. The playwrights corrected Hall in
one particular in which he had depicted More on
the day of his execution as mocking the poor
woman who asked for the return of her court
papers which were before him when he was Chan-
cellor. In the play More asks her forgiveness
and she responds by saying that he was the best
friend the poor ever had. Chambers points out
that More, the Catholic martyr, is remembered
by Protestant London as "a special lover and
friend in the businesses and causes of this
city" (p. 46).

104 Chambrun, Clara Longworth de. *Shakespeare Re-
      discovered.* New York: Scribner's, 1938.
      Chap. 13, "The Book of Sir Thomas More,"
      pp. 280-90.

   Reviews the history of the manuscript and
the scholarship on the play. She cites the
presence of Goodal's name and parallels between
Addition IIc and Shakespeare's acknowledged
plays in support of his authorship of the Addition, accepts the opinion of certain scholars
that the play includes political propaganda
favoring Essex, and assigns it a date close to
the Essex rebellion.

105 Chambers, R. W. "Shakespeare and the Play of
      More." *Man's Unconquerable Mind.* London:
      Cape, 1939. Reprint. New York: Haskell,

1967. Pp. 204-49. In its original form
this essay appeared in *Shakespeare's Hand in
the Play of Sir Thomas More* edited by A. W.
Pollard, Cambridge: Cambridge University
Press, 1923. In recast form it was printed
in part in *Modern Language Review*, 26 (1931):
251-80, and delivered in part as the Ludwig
Mond Lecture at the University of Manchester
in 1937. In this new summary version Chambers takes into account work done by others
since 1923, especially that of Spurgeon (item
98), and proposes "to approach the problem
yet again, ... from a somewhat different
angle" (p. 210).

Sets forth the proposition that the literary
evidence for the identification of the author
of the 147 lines written in hand D in *Sir Thomas
More* can only be brought to bear on the question
by an examination of the ideas in the context
in which they occur. The ideas underlying
More's speech to the rioting craftsmen are passionate abhorrence of mob rule, good natured
ridicule of mob logic, and a belief in the essential goodness of humble folk. This combination is recognizably Shakespearean but more
important is the fact that these same ideas
occur in acknowledged plays, are expressed in
essentially similar ways and even in the same
sequence in the mob scenes in *2 Henry IV,
Julius Caesar* and *Coriolanus* and in Ulysses'
speech on degree in *Troilus*. Shakespeare's
abiding concern about the destructiveness of
revolt against kingly authority is most memor-
ably expressed, as one might expect, in *Richard
II*. In *Sir Thomas More* a similar concern is
implicit in More's speech in which he employs
a series of figures of similar import to those
used in *Richard II*--e.g. rebellion is a flooding
river overflowing its natural bounds. These
images sometimes occur in the work of other
playwrights; but not in almost the same circumstances and not so consistently interrelated.
"This rhythm of thought produced ... in the
'three pages' and in Shakespeare, sequences
running to four, five, six, or seven elements"
(p. 249). Parallelism of thought, supported
by all the other evidence, leads to the con-

clusion that Shakespeare is far more likely
to be the source of hand D than any other
contemporary playwright.

106 Crundell, H. W. "Shakespeare and the Play of
     More," *Times Literary Supplement*, 20 May
     1939, pp. 297-8.

     Points out that in More's soliloquy on
     greatness (Addition III) in *Sir Thomas More*
     he refers to "corruption of the blood" that
     could occur unless he as Lord Chancellor is
     careful to observe due respect in his relations
     with his father. This term is usually applied
     to serious crimes such as treason. Similar
     ideas are expressed, employing similar terms,
     in *King Lear* and *Julius Caesar*. This additional
     evidence bearing on the Shakespearean author-
     ship of Addition III supports the case for his
     authorship of Addition IIc. See item 107.

107 Chambers, R. W. "Shakespeare and More," *Times
     Literary Supplement*, 3 June 1939, p. 327.

     Agrees that the new evidence presented by
     Crundell (item 106) strengthens the attribution
     to Shakespeare of Addition III of the *Sir
     Thomas More* manuscript and lends additional
     support to his claim to Addition IIc. Any evi-
     dence pointing to distinctive Shakespearean
     passages in hands other than D strengthens the
     case for the belief that Shakespeare partici-
     pated in writing the play and that he is the
     author of the 147 lines.

108 Doran, Madeleine. "An Evaluation of Evidence
     in Shakespearean Textual Criticism," *English
     Institute Annual 1941*. New York: Columbia
     University Press, 1942. Pp. 105-7.

     Disputes efforts to identify Shakespearean
     quarto copy as autograph because it tends to
     employ circular reasoning: spelling and punc-
     tuation of the quartos identify Hand D of *Sir
     Thomas More* as Shakespeare's; then Hand D is
     used to establish patterns in the quartos as
     autograph. Emphasizes that the lightness of

the punctuation common in Shakespeare does not constitute proof of anything because there have not been enough studies of the punctuation of non-Shakespearean plays.

109 Deutschberger, Paul. "Shakspere and *Sir Thomas Moore*," *Shakespeare Association Bulletin*, 18 (1943): 75-91, 99-108, 156-67.

Attacks both the case for identification of Hand D in *Sir Thomas More* as Shakespeare's and for his authorship of Addition IIc. There are two lines of argument: aesthetic and paleographical. Neither stands scrutiny. If Shakespeare had contributed to *Sir Thomas More* there would be at least some tradition to that effect but there is none. The character and quality of the scene do not give assurances concerning its authorship. The ideas, especially the political ideas, to which Chambers (item 105) calls attention in Addition IIc are commonplace and provide no means of identifying the writer. A comparison of the scene with Ulysses' speech on degree demonstrates more important differences than parallels and both are mere rewordings of conventional themes. Of the twelve images that occur in the scene thought by Spurgeon (item 98) to be characteristic of Shakespeare seven are of no value as evidence because they consist of a single word and three of the remaining five are merely conventional. Close comparison of the *Sir Thomas More* phrase "law in liom" with a similar phrase in *Coriolanus* shows that it is not the same image. The ravenous fishes image is very old, common in Elizabethan times and no proof of Shakespeare's hand. Both Chambers's and Spurgeon's arguments may be dismissed. Thompson acknowledges that Hand D does not compare closely to Shakespeare's signatures. This he explains as due to the passage of time and the fact that Shakespeare had writer's cramp, but neurologists who have studied the signatures find no evidence of writer's cramp. The so-called peculiarities of letter formation are duplicated in hundreds of manuscripts. Sir Edward's case is unscientific, inconsequential and illogical.

110 Flatter, Richard. "Eine Szene in Shakespeares
    Handschrift," *Neue Auslese* 2:6 (1947): 61-6.

Reviews the history of the *Sir Thomas More*
manuscript and scholarship, concluding that
Addition IIc, in spite of the paucity of authenticated Shakespearean handwriting available as
a control, is in Shakespeare's hand, and that
the sentiments and thought of the scenes are
Shakespearean. It is truly his humanitarian
voice. Photographic facsimiles of five lines
of the manuscript and of Shakespeare's signa-
ture on the third page of his will, and a translation into German of Addition IIc, are included.

111 Bald, R. C. "*The Booke of Sir Thomas More* and
    its Problems," *Shakespeare Survey* 2 (1949):
    44-61. Reprint. *Evidence for Authorship:
    Essays on Problems of Attribution*. Edited
    by David V. Erdman and Ephim G. Fogel.
    Ithaca: Cornell University Press, 1966.
    Item 29.

Lucidly summarizes and evaluates the state
of *Sir Thomas More* scholarship to 1948, reex-
amining the arguments pro and con for the identification of Hand D as Shakespeare's in the
several disciplines employed--palaeographic,
bibliographic, literary. Bald endorses Greg's
conclusive opinion that the palaeographic case
for the two hands being the same is stronger
than any case that can be made out for their
being different. Wilson's arguments from
spellings--especially the apparently unique
scilens--are found cumulatively forceful, and
Bald presents two small spelling discoveries of
his own. Although some of the details of the
arguments for identifying Hand D as Shakespeare's
have not borne the scrutiny of adverse critics,
the essential case made by Pollard, Greg,
Wilson, Thompson and R. W. Chambers in 1923
remains intact and in some aspects has been
strengthened by Spurgeon (item 98) and by
Chambers's revision to his original essay. If
the positive case is not conclusive, the argument from elimination establishes Shakespeare
as D especially from a literary point of view

since the only other possible candidates are
Marlowe, Chapman and Jonson whose distinctive
voices are in no case that of Addition IIc.
If the identity of D as Shakespeare is accepted,
then from stylistic evidence he must also be the
author of Addition III (More's greatness soliloquy). As to date of composition almost every
date from 1586 to 1604 has been suggested.
Heywood began writing plays about 1596, Chettle
and Dekker in 1598. Verse parallels between
Sir Thomas More and *Julius Caesar* and *Troilus*
point to a slightly later date, perhaps 1600.
The Essex troubles would have made Tilney extra-
cautious at that time about approving a play
showing an insurrection. During the middle of
1600 the Admiral's Men went on tour, the Fortune
was being built and Henslowe was less than usually active in securing new plays. Munday and
his associates were then free to offer their
play to the Lord Chamberlain's Men and when revisions became necessary Shakespeare could have
taken a hand. On this hypothesis *Sir Thomas
More* was begun in the latter part of 1600.

112 Stirling, Brents. *The Populace in Shakespeare.*
New York: Columbia University Press, 1949.

Notes that the behavior of the mob in *Sir
Thomas More* is the least unruly in all Eliza-
bethan drama with the relationship between the
London craftsmen and More most cordial (157-9).
Questions Shakespearean participation.

113 Schücking, Levin L. "Uber einige Probleme der
Neueren und Neuesten Shakespeare--Forschung:
(Textgestaltung und Echtheitsfragen),"
Germanisch-romanische Monatsschrift, 33
(1951-2): 208-28.

Reasserts in the latter part of this essay
(pp. 225-8) the position originally set forth
in his 1925 paper ("Shakespeare and *Sir Thomas
More*," *Review of English Studies*, 1 [1925]:
40-59) regarding Shakespeare's possible authorship of Addition IIc of *Sir Thomas More* (Schücking rejects Shakespeare and favors Heywood);
and his suggested date of composition which he
places at c. 1601 because he associates *Sir*

Thomas More with 1 and 2 *Cardinal Wolsey* and
Thomas Lord Cromwell in a loose tetralogy.
Chettle, Heywood and Munday form the connecting
thread. Both of Schücking's hypotheses have
been rejected by E. K. Chambers (item 2, 1:
509 and 513), by R. W. Chambers (item 105, pp.
233-9) and by Greg (item 16, p. 99).

114 Feuillerat, Albert. *The Composition of Shake-
speare's Plays: Authorship, Chronology.*
New Haven: Yale University Press, 1953.
Pp. 48-9 n.

Rejects the identification of Hand D in the
Sir Thomas More manuscript as Shakespeare's because it has characteristics that are opposite
to those revealed in the authenticated signatures. Possibly it is the hand of a scrivener.

115 Maas, Paul. "Henry Finch and Shakespeare,"
Review of English Studies, n.s. 4 (1953):
142.

Quotes from a debate in Parliament on 21 and
23 March, 1593 part of a speech by Henry Finch,
then Member for Canterbury, in which he opposes
a bill prohibiting aliens from selling commod-
ities and speaks in favor of the "strangers,"
including the phrase "we may be strangers here-
after, so let us do as we would be done unto"
(p. 142). Compares this to the passage in *Sir
Thomas More* in which More draws a hypothetical
picture of the rebels as strangers in a foreign
land and they respond:
  fayth a saies trewe letts do as we may be
doon by
                              (141 of Add. IIc)

116 Hyde, Mary C., comp. "Current Theater Notes."
Shakespeare Quarterly, 6 (1955): 67-88.

Lists an arena production of *Sir Thomas More*
by The Theatre Center London 22 to 29 June 1954,
presented in Elizabethan dress 22-25 June, in
modern dress 26-29 June. Directed by Brian Way
with Michael Beint in the title role. See
item 120.

117 Nosworthy, J. M.   "Shakespeare and *Sir Thomas
     More*," *Review of English Studies*, n.s. 6
     (1955): 12-25.

     The additions to *Sir Thomas More* are theat-
     rical in inspiration and aim at elimination of
     inferior matter, reduction in the size of the
     cast and heightening of dramatic effect. The
     notion that Shakespeare was commissioned to
     supply material that would be acceptable to the
     authorities is untenable. The collaboration of
     Munday, Chettle and Dekker points to a date in
     the range of 1597-1601 in consideration of the
     nine plays dated from 1598 to 1602 in which the
     three participated. Lexical evidence in Ad-
     dition IIc clearly displays affinity with
     Shakespeare's middle plays, pointing to a date
     c. 1601-2. The vocabulary of Addition III and
     its thematic content, especially the relation-
     ship of God and man and the child's obligation
     to the parent, is manifestly Shakespearean, found
     throughout the canon and notably in such middle
     plays as *Henry IV, Hamlet, Lear* and *Troilus.*
     Addition IIc and Addition III are entirely con-
     cordant. The conclusion is that Munday, Chettle
     and Dekker wrote *Sir Thomas More* about 1600 and
     that Shakespeare wrote Additions IIc and III
     about 1601-2.

118 Maxwell, Baldwin. *Studies in the Shakespeare
     Apocrypha.* New York: King's Crown Press,
     1956, pp. 103-8.

     Describes the relationship of *Sir Thomas
     More* to *Thomas Lord Cromwell* primarily in re-
     gard to the "long-haired ruffian" incident.
     Foxe's *Acts and Monuments* relates it as happen-
     ing to Cromwell, but it is told of More in
     Sir Thomas More and is absent from the play
     Thomas Lord Cromwell.

119 Nosworthy, J. M.   "Hand B in *Sir Thomas More*,"
     The Library, fifth series 11 (1956): 47-50.

     Reviews the designation of Hand B in *Sir
     Thomas More* as Heywood's in the light of the
     recent publication of the Malone Society's

edition of *The Captives* including an analysis
of Heywood's handwriting by the editor, Arthur
Brown. Hand B has certain features in common
with Heywood's hand but the differences are
even more noteworthy. Habits of letter formation, capitalization and spelling are significantly divergent. On the whole Tannenbaum's
identification of B as Heywood is unsatisfactory
and if B is not Heywood's hand neither is it
that of any other known Elizabethan dramatist.
There is nothing in the play that can be confidently ascribed to Heywood on the grounds of
style or treatment.

120 Shakespeare Memorial Library, Birmingham.
      "Shakespeare Productions in the United King-
      dom: 1954." *Shakespeare Survey*, 9 (1956):
      120.

      Lists 1954 production of *Sir Thomas More* by
      The Theatre Center, London, sponsored by Donald
      Wolfit on behalf of Advance Players Association,
      Ltd., produced by Douglas Seale. See item 116.

121 Lane, Ralph H. "Shakespearean Spelling."
      Shakespeare Newsletter, 8:4 (September 1958):
      28.

      Analyzes spelling in twenty-two books pub-
      lished in 1600, including *Much Ado, 2 Henry IV,
      Midsummer Night's Dream* and *Merchant of Venice*
      comprising 40,000 words. Only 47% varied from
      modern practice. Of 377 spellings authentically
      Shakespearean in the four plays, seventy-seven
      are distinctive, the majority followed standard
      current usage. A comparison of the spellings
      in Addition IIc with those in the four 1600
      quartos shows that the spellings of the *Sir
      Thomas More* fragment fail in important details
      to match the spellings of the quartos. Seventy-
      eight forms vary while 125 are the same but
      only four are impressive: *doon, Iarman, hurly*
      and *scilens*. If the control list from the four
      quartos is valid it disqualifies Shakespeare as
      the penman who wrote Hand D.

122 MacNalty, Arthur Salusbury. "Shakespeare and
      Sir Thomas More," *Essays and Studies*, new
      series 12 (1959): 36-57.

      Describes the influence of More on Shakespeare
as seen in *Richard III*, both parts of *Henry IV*,
Henry V and *Sir Thomas More*. In a section of
his essay entitled "The Play of *Sir Thomas More*"
(pp. 37-46) MacNalty traces the history and
scholarship of *Sir Thomas More* from Dyce's
edition to Tillyard (item 13). He finds evidence of Shakespeare's style in several passages
other than Additions IIc and III, and thinks
that Shakespeare's alterations may have been
more extensive than is generally accepted, especially in the interpretation of the central
character. He surmises that Munday and his fellow playwrights turned to Shakespeare for assistance because they knew of his interest in More
and speculates that Shakespeare may have been
contemplating a play on More. On the basis of
the mention of the actor Goodale he conjectures
that the play was performed but perhaps only
once, for the subject was politically and re-
ligiously thorny while Anne Boleyn's daughter
was on the throne.

123 Huber, R. A. "On Looking over Shakespeare's
      'Secretarie,'" *Stratford Papers on Shake-
      speare 1960*. Edited by B. A. W. Jackson.
      Toronto: Gage, 1961. Pp. 53-70. Preceded
      by an Editor's note (pp. 52-3) and followed
      by a Postscript by C. J. Sisson (pp. 70-7).

      Employs "scientific" handwriting analysis
techniques used by the Royal Canadian Mounted
Police of whose crime detection laboratory
Staff Sergeant Huber is the head. He is also
internationally recognized as an authority on
the authentication of disputed documents. Reviewing the evidence for the identification in
the *Sir Thomas More* manuscript of Hand D as
Shakespeare's marshalled by Thompson and Greg,
he proposes to test identification on the basis
of a three-step procedure: 1--analysis of the
features of Hand D; 2--comparison of the Hand
with the authentic signatures; and 3--evalua-

tion of the significance of the findings generated by the comparison. Hand D shows many signs
of similarity to Shakespeare's acknowledged
handwriting but there are a number of salient
differences that cannot be adequately accounted
for by assuming physical infirmity or by the
passage of time. On the other hand the evidence for opposing Shakespeare's authorship is
limited to inconsistencies that are not necessarily true or significant dissimilarities.
Shakespeare is one of a small group of writers
who could have written Hand D but the evidence
is not sufficiently strong to justify a positive identification. The present study is seriously impaired by being restricted to the examination of photographic reproductions.

Sisson notes the legitimate bounds of Huber's
study (limited to handwriting analysis) and the
serious burden of working from reproductions,
and summarizes the steps he has taken in his
own inquiries: 1--general view of the writing
as a whole; 2--analysis of the style of writing;
3--detailed analysis of the forms of letters;
4--identification of idiosyncrasies of letter
forms or penwork; 5--examination of ancillary
internal evidence. Of all the evidence, two
pieces are of primary importance: the form of
the "spurred a" and the spelling *scilens*. In
forty years of reading an estimated half a mil-
lion sheets of contemporary manuscripts Sisson
finds that these forms have not been duplicated.
He concurs however in the general opinion of
scholar-paleographers that the identification
of Hand D cannot rest on handwriting analysis
alone.

124 Jenkins, Harold. "A Supplement to Sir Walter
      Greg's Edition of *Sir Thomas More*," *Malone
      Society Collections*, 6 (1961): 177-92. Re-
      print in 1961 issue of Greg's 1911 edition.

      Notes that the identification of the various
      hands in the manuscript (other than Tilney's)
      has settled with varying degrees of certainty
      to be: S--Anthony Munday; A--Henry Chettle;
      B--Thomas Heywood; C--a playhouse bookkeeper;
      D--William Shakespeare; E--Thomas Dekker. Of
      these only B as Heywood (not improbable) and D

(Shakespeare) have been subject to any doubt.
That D is Shakespeare is likely because the
combination of resemblances of handwriting,
spelling and sequences in the development of
ideas outstrips any credible coincidence. Jenkins agrees with Bald (item 99) that if Addition
IIc in Hand D is Shakespeare's, then Addition
III (More's soliloquy) is Shakespeare's also.
Munday is accepted as the principal author of
the original play, but his scribal error *fashis*
supports the idea that *Sir Thomas More* was a
collaboration from the beginning. Munday's absence from the revisions is odd as is the fact
that the revisions do not respond to Tilney's
strictures. Sir Edmund Chambers's explanation
of the sequence of events seems best: Tilney
read and censored the original version which
was set aside to be taken up later and revised
but not again submitted for license. The problem of the date is complex. The comparative
youth of Dekker and Heywood is not relevant unless it can be shown they were part of the
original collaboration. Munday's hand in *Sir
Thomas More* is known to fall between authenticated writings of 1590 and 1602 but closer to
the earlier date. A date at about 1600-1601
would take account of the emergence of Dekker
and Chettle as playwrights and accords with the
affinities of Addition IIc with Shakespeare's
great tragedies and *Coriolanus*. But the playhouse scribe (C), who went over D's three pages,
was associated with the Admiral's Men by 1597
and it is hard to believe that Shakespeare was
engaged in revising a play for the major rival
of the Chamberlain's Company. C had been associated with Strange's about 1590 and may have
left them when Strange's became the Lord Chamberlain's in 1594. The conjunction of Hands C
and D makes a date before 1594 likely. This
squares with Pollard's view that the riot scenes
could not have been presented after the riots of
1595 and the subsequent savage executions. Top-
ical allusions are of little help. The dates
that best fit the evidence are c. 1590-3 for the
original composition and c. 1594-5 for the revision. The state of the manuscript does not
argue against performance because a usable

prompt-book could have been developed by a clean
transcription. Jenkins appends a list of revised readings which mostly deal with spelling.

125 Shapiro, I. A. "Shakespeare and Mundy," *Shake-
      speare Survey*, 14 (1961): 25-33.

      Believes Meres's description of Mundy as the
best plotter meant not only that he devised
clever plots but also that he was a provider
of plots on the basis of which other writers
composed plays. The payment made to him by
Henslowe on 2 December 1602 of £3 for *The Set
at Tennis* could not have been for a complete
play and must have been for a plot. Is it possible, Shapiro asks, that some such plots originally used for *Leir* and *The Famous Victories*
were re-used by Shakespeare as the plots for
King Lear and *Henry V*? The original draft of
Sir Thomas More was Mundy's. It is difficult
to establish Shakespeare's connection with the
revision. The paleographic evidence is inconclusive. It is more profitable to consider
what Shakespeare may have learned from Mundy's
contribution to the play. Mundy's achievement
exhibits the same kind of skill and insight in
handling source material that we admire in
Shakespeare. In 1593 Mundy could hardly have
learned this from Shakespeare, though Shakespeare may have learned it from Mundy. In consideration of his strong anti-Catholic bias
his magnanimous appreciation of More, the Catholic martyr, may have had no little influence on
Shakespeare's rendering of history in subsequent
plays.

126 Bradbrook, M. C. *The Rise of the Common Player:
      A Study of Actor and Society in Shakespeare's
      England*. London: Chatto and Windus, 1962.
      Reprint. Cambridge: Cambridge University
      Press, 1979. Pp. 51, 127, 234, 291, 294, 300.

      Cites activities of Lord Cardinal's players
in *Sir Thomas More* as evidence of social and
economic status of common players in Tudor
times.

127 Brinkman, Karl and Wolfgang Clemen. "Inter-
    national Notes: Germany," *Shakespeare
    Survey*, 15 (1962): 134.

    Richard Flatter's attempt to combine the
    Shakespearean portions of *Henry VIII* and *Sir
    Thomas More* into a single play acted in Germany
    in 1960 lacks dramatic unity and fails to be
    more than a loose sequence of historical pag-
    eants.

128 Styan, J. L. "Dwarfed by Shakespeare? In
    Search of an Elizabethan Heritage," *Plays
    and Players* (July 1964): 8-12.

    Discusses a season of Elizabethan and Jaco-
    bean plays by various acting companies includ-
    ing a production of *Sir Thomas More* at the
    Nottingham playhouse.

129 Livermore, Ann. "Shakespeare and St. Augus-
    tine," *Quarterly Review*, 644 (April 1965):
    181-93.

    Identifies Augustinian thought in several
    of Shakespeare's plays including *Sir Thomas
    More*. More's speech to the mob follows an in-
    junction by St. Augustine to modify oratory to
    the mood of the hearers. Shakespeare may have
    incorporated Augustinian thinking into plays
    he was reworking to elevate their tone and sig-
    nificance and to deepen their moral seriousness.

130 Nosworthy, J. M. *Shakespeare's Occasional
    Plays*. London: Arnold, 1965.

    Accepts implicitly the Shakespearean author-
    ship of the insurrection scene in *Sir Thomas
    More* by employing *passim* such aspects of the
    manuscript as spellings and punctuation to il-
    luminate textual problems of canonical plays.
    In Appendix 1, "Alternative Endings," Nos-
    worthy discusses such endings in connection
    with *Timon*, *Faustus* and *Sir Thomas More*, noting
    that the long addition by Chettle to the *More*
    manuscript could constitute an alternative end-
    ing. He cites a comment in a private letter by

Ellis-Fermor who, after seeing a performance of
Sir Thomas More, expressed the conviction that
the manuscript preserves three distinct endings
(p. 226).

131 Walton, J. K. "The Year's Contribution to
Shakespearian Studies: Textual Studies,"
Shakespeare Survey, 20 (1967): 170-9.

In the course of a review (pp. 173-4) of A.
R. Humphrey's text of *2 Henry VI* in his New
Arden edition, Walton cites Greg's earlier statement that the three pages of *Sir Thomas More*
fairly represent the foul papers that Shakespeare habitually turned over to his company.
Walton counts the number of errors and anomalies in the 172 lines of the *Sir Thomas More*
fragment and extrapolates them for the 3446
lines of *2 Henry VI*, showing that the number
of projected errors and anomalies thus determined is much greater than can be demonstrated
to be present in fact in the Folio text of *2
Henry VI*. Thus the problem becomes not why the
errors and anomalies are so many but why they
are so few. He also notes that the state of
Addition IIc would lead us to believe that in
a Shakespearean manuscript the substantive
errors and anomalies are mainly graphic.

132 Bentley, Gerald Eades. *The Profession of Dra-
matist in Shakespeare's Time, 1590-1642*.
Princeton: Princeton University Press, 1971.
P. 174.

Notes the significance of *Sir Thomas More* in
the system of stage regulation and censorship,
concluding that "it is not clear that the manuscript was ever thoroughly rewritten" as Tilney
required or that the play was ever performed.

133 Blayney, Peter W. M. *"The Booke of Sir Thomas
Moore* Re-Examined," *Studies in Philology*, 69
(1972): 167-91.

Speculates that the state of the manuscript
of *Sir Thomas More* results from two separate
submissions to Tilney, the Master of the Revels,

and two distinct stages of revision. On the
occasion of the first submission Tilney objected primarily to the prentices protest. In the
course of the revision to meet this objection
Shakespeare wrote the new insurrection scene,
the clown's part was added and some literary
deletions were replaced by new material. The
revised play was submitted a second time to
Tilney but again returned, this time with an
instruction to delete the insurrection scenes,
a more far reaching objection. Another attempt
was made to revise the play but the effort was
abandoned either because it was realized that
approval was unlikely or because of an outbreak
of the plague. The objective evidence for dating the manuscript is limited to the time when
Tilney was Master of the Revels, Thomas Goodal
was a Chamberlain's man, Ogle was a theatrical
supplier and Dekker and Heywood were writing
plays. Echoes of *Sir Thomas More* in Chettle's
Kind-Harts Dream (1592) and especially the use
of some twenty unusual words from Addition IIc
imply that he knew *Sir Thomas More* between September and November, 1592. The progress of
events was therefore on this order: May-June
1592: *Sir Thomas More* plotted, perhaps by Munday, the scenes drafted by several playwrights
and submitted to Tilney; June-August: Tilney,
influenced by recent unrest, objected to scenes
of prentice riots and street brawls and returned the manuscript; August-November: revisions made and new material written by Chettle, Heywood, Shakespeare and the playhouse
reviser (Hand C) and resubmitted to Tilney;
December 1592-January 1593: Tilney then objected to the Ill May Day episode as a whole;
revisions are again attempted but the effort
is abandoned in the spring of 1593.

Blayney points out some aspects of the manuscript not previously noted: the verso of
Folio 9 is not blank but contains the word *all*
and the smudged beginning of another word; Munday's participation is probably less than previously thought; and pen nib strokes indicate
that Chettle was left-handed.

134 Gaskell, Philip. *A New Introduction to Biblio-*
     graphy. Oxford: Oxford University Press,

1972. P. 359.

In a discussion of the editorial treatment of accidentals in dramatic texts Gaskell cites twenty lines from Addition IIc of the manuscript of *Sir Thomas More* which he describes as an extreme case of a challenge to an editor to make sense of "spelling and capitalization [that] are wildly inconsistent and punctuation [that] is largely absent." He advocates honoring the author's intentions but not to the extent of "reproducing the manifest inadequacies of his accidentals."

135 Bergeron, David M. "Shakespeare and Munday Again," *American Notes & Queries*, 12:3 (October 1973): 28-32.

Notes that Munday, being Shakespeare's senior by four years, may have influenced the greater poet. Scholars recently have determined that his romance *Zelauto* was probably one of the sources of *Merchant of Venice* (Stillinger) and possibly of *Two Gentlemen of Verona* (Wright), and that Munday in *Sir Thomas More* may have helped shape Shakespeare's approach to history plays (Shapiro). See item 125.

136 Wentersdorf, Karl P. "Linkages of Thought and Imagery in Shakespeare and *More*," *Modern Language Quarterly*, 34 (1973): 384-505.

Adds a sixth image, that of the cruelty of pagans and savages, to the five pointed out by R. W. Chambers (item 105) in his essay on the Shakespearean images in *Sir Thomas More* Addition IIc, and shows that the five sequences of thought and imagery defined by Chambers (violation of order, flood images, defenselessness of the aged and young, monsters and cannibals, supplicants using their knees as feet) and found in *Richard II*, *Hamlet*, *King Lear*, *Troilus* and *Coriolanus* also occur, sometimes in incomplete form, in *King John*, *2 Henry IV*, *Henry V*, *Julius Caesar*, *Macbeth*, *Othello* and *Timon* as well as in *Sir Thomas More*. The new image to which attention is called for the first time occurs in *Sir Thomas More* and ten other

times in nine plays (*Richard II*, *King John*,
2 Henry IV, *Henry V*, *Julius Caesar*, *King Lear*,
Macbeth, *Othello* and *Coriolanus*). This striking and unusual linkage of ideas is distinctive
and may even be exclusively Shakespearean.
Chambers's original claim that it is highly
characteristic of Shakespeare is strengthened
by its twenty appearances in the canon (p. 402).

137 Spikes, Judith Doolin. "*The Book of Sir Thomas
     More*: Structure and Meaning," *Moreana*, 11:3
     (1974): 25-39.

Argues that *Sir Thomas More* exhibits greater
thematic and structural unity than critics
credit it with. The first half of the play is
concerned with social and political responsibility, the second half with the moral law which
supersedes man's law. The two parts are bal-
anced around a central section which states the
problem abstractly, first in the form of a med-
itative soliloquy, then concretely in the moral
allegory of the interpolated play. All of the
play's episodes are designed to reflect or to
elaborate upon some aspect of this theme. The
two members of the King's privy council who
are troubled by Henry's assumption of eccle-
siastical supremacy react in different ways.
John Fisher, Bishop of Rochester, saw the issue
in terms of loyalties due to earthly and heaven-
ly sovereigns. He refused to subscribe to the
articles and was immediately arrested. For
More the issue is a conflict between conscience
and comfort, between the spiritual and physical;
between, in the terms of the allegory, Wisdom
and Vanity. More resigned the Chancellorship
and asked for time to think, but he ultimately
chooses conscience rather than ease, specifi-
cally rejecting the dominance of mere Fortune
in human affairs and, in the first line of his
soliloquy, says heaven directs man. *Sir Thomas
More* is a complex examination of the issue of
responsibility, the central theme of the play,
expressed through diverse episodic actions in
the manner of interior duplication, each action
elaborating a different aspect of the issue.

138 Bradbrook, M. C. "The Triple Bond: Audience, Actors, Author in the Elizabethan Playhouse." *The Triple Bond*, edited by Joseph G. Price. University Park, Pennsylvania: Pennsylvania State University Press, 1975. Pp. 52-3.

Cites as one evidence of the triple bond the interaction of More and the players of my Lord Cardinal in *Sir Thomas More*. The play, "fated never to reach the boards" (p. 52), shows that the players had a lively sense of their own history.

139 Hays, Michael L. "Shakespeare's Hand in *Sir Thomas More*: Some Aspects of the Paleographic Argument," *Shakespeare Studies*, 8 (1975): 241-53.

Asserts the fundamental need for adequate factual information to determine the identity of the writer of Hand D in the manuscript *Sir Thomas More*. The paucity of data available to establish Shakespeare's hand means that any determination is conjectural. Shakespeare's signatures do not constitute a reliable control because they are official in function while Hand D is literary. Only in respect of the general sort of hand is a similarity between the control (Shakespeare's) and the unknown hand (Hand D) established. Any effort to argue either the similarity or dissimilarity of the hands must be inconclusive because the evidence is insufficient. Since there are significant differences among the signatures and no external authentication exists, the control evidence may not only be insufficient; it may not even exist. In these circumstances no argument for attribution on paleographic grounds is possible. See item 183.

140 Hunter, G. K. "Were There Act-Pauses on Shakespeare's Stage?" *English Renaissance Drama: Essays in Honor of Madeleine Doran and Mark Eccles*. Edited by Standish Henning, Robert Kimbrough, Richard Knowles. Carbondale: Southern Illinois University Press, 1976. Pp. 23-4.

Studies four manuscript plays for evidence
of the presence or lack of act-pauses on the
Globe stage: *Sir Thomas More*, *Edmond Ironside*,
Richard II / Thomas of Woodstock and *John a Kent
and John a Cumber*. Hunter concludes with Greg
that the manuscript of *Sir Thomas More* is anom-
alous in many ways and that the absence of act
divisions indicates that the play was not seriously prepared for the stage.

141 Ramsey, Paul. "Shakespeare and *Sir Thomas More*
        Revisited: or, A Mounty on the Trail,"
        *Papers of the Bibliographical Society of
        America*, 70 (1976): 333-46.

        Reviews the evidence of Pollard, Greg, Thomp-
son, Wilson and Chambers, identifying Hand D in
the *Sir Thomas More* manuscript as Shakespeare's,
in the light of Huber's findings (item 123)
under the headings of the paleographical, orthographical, literary and metrical cases for
identification. The contributors to *Shakespeare's Hand in the Play of Sir Thomas More*,
who demonstrate according to Ramsey a *parti
pris* approach, do not deal with the weaknesses
in their case nor with the evidence that shows
differences between Hand D and Shakespeare's
writing. Thompson's paleographic presentation
is particularly weak in this regard as Huber
has shown. Ramsey quotes Huber's conclusion
that the evidence is insufficient to confirm or
deny that the writing in Hand D is Shakespeare's.
Most of the rest of the evidence is conjectural
and in many instances either weak or suscept-
ible to different interpretation. The paleographic case is weak and slightly negative; the
orthographic case is slightly favorable especially on the basis of *scilens* and *straing*; the
literary case, resting as it does on commonplaces, is somewhat negative; the metrical evidence is inconclusive; and the rhythmical evidence is against identification. Ramsey's impression is that D is not Shakespeare, yet there
remains a reasonable doubt.

142 Long, William B. "False Expectations: The Con-
        sequences of Ignoring Manuscripts," *Shake-
        speare Newsletter*, 27 (1977): 15.

Proposes a thorough re-examination of the
sixteen extant playbooks of the Shakespearean
era to 1642 to increase scholarly knowledge of
the practical theatre history of the period.
Long cites the illuminating facts to be derived
from a comprehensive study of the manuscript of
Sir Thomas More concerning what was done to the
manuscript in the theatre in preparation for
production.

143 Matchett, William H. "Shylock, Iago, and *Sir
    Thomas More*: With Some Further Discussion
    of Shakespeare's Imagination," *PMLA*, 92
    (1977): 217-30.

Cites in *Othello* and *Sir Thomas More* associations from *The Merchant of Venice* that are
linguistic, imagistic and conceptual in nature,
including those noted in the staging as well as
the text, demonstrating the presence of fundamentally abstract ideas common to all three
plays that assume related but different forms
in each play. Since these associated thoughts
are diffused throughout *The Merchant of Venice*,
but concentrated in *Othello* and *Sir Thomas More*,
they first came together in Shakespeare's imagination in the course of composition of *Merchant
of Venice*. The clustered associations derived
from that play that appear in Addition IIc of
Sir Thomas More constitute another argument for
Shakespeare's authorship. Since the priority
of date of *Merchant of Venice* is assumed,
Matchett favors a date for *Sir Thomas More* of
c. 1600. Similar associations of ideas occur
in other Shakespearean plays, analysis of which
may be helpful in solving other problems of
date. More important is the demonstration of a
wide-ranging mental process making available to
the artistic imagination flexible systems of
intermeshing concepts growing out of Shakespeare's whole past.

144 Petti, Anthony G. *English Literary Hands from
    Chaucer to Dryden*. Cambridge, Mass.: Harvard
    University Press, 1977. Pp. 87, 91, 95 and
    111.

Includes facsimiles of folios 9 and 13 of

British Library MS. Harleian 7368 (*Sir Thomas
More*); of folio 54 of British Library MS.
Edgerton 1994 (Heywood's *The Captives*); and of
folio 31 of Dulwich College Henslowe's Diary
MS. 7 exhibiting Hands D, C, B and A of the
Sir Thomas More manuscript. Petti provides a
brief description of the kind of hand-writing,
a transcript and notes, including a general
discussion of the hands in connection with the
Sir Thomas More manuscript, characteristics,
punctuation and abbreviation. Identification
of Hand D as Shakespeare's rests on slender
paleographic evidence (general impression and a
few distinctive forms) but is supported by
other evidence and the case is generally held
sufficiently proved. Hand C bears a resemblance to Hand D but Greg identified it as that
of a playhouse scribe. Paleographic evidence
shows that C is somewhat more likely to be
Dekker who has been identified with Hand E.
Hand B is possibly but not certainly Heywood's.
Hand A is Chettle.

145 Leek, Robert - H. "A Year of Shakespeare in
      Kiwiland." *Shakespeare Quarterly*, 30 (1979):
      272-7.

      Included in a season of seven Shakespearean
productions in New Zealand (1978) was a presentation of *Sir Thomas More* at the Mayfair Theatre,
Dunedin in a text edited by Alistair Fox directed by Jane Oakshott both of the English Department of Otago University. Five performances
were given by an ad hoc amateur company of
fifty-five actors. There was praise for the
production and for Ern Joyce in the title role
in spite of the weakness of the play and the
unevenness of the cast.

146 Chillington, Carol A. "Playwrights at Work:
      Henslowe's, Not Shakespeare's, *Book of Sir
      Thomas More*," *English Literary Renaissance*,
      10:3 (Autumn, 1980): 439-79.

      Determines that only an especially threaten-
ing event could have called forth from the
censor so absolute an injunction as Tilney's
prohibition noted at the beginning of *Sir*

Thomas More. Following Collins (item 152) and
Bald (item 111) and taking into account the
lexical affinities between *Sir Thomas More* and
Shakespeare's mature plays Chillington settles
on a date for the play after the Essex rebellion. Pollard's aphorism that a late date would
be fatal to Shakespeare's participation is
pressed into service in support of an hypothesis that *Sir Thomas More* is the product of Henslowe's "theatrical industry" (p. 445). Chillington traces the numerous transactions between Henslowe and his playwrights, particularly Chettle, Heywood, Dekker and Munday, and
points out that play revisions occurred usually
only on the revivals of old plays. The alterations in *Sir Thomas More* are of a different
type and were made shortly after the original
composition. Henslowe's records demonstrate
that the competition between rival companies
was fierce and Shakespeare would hardly have
been willing to redeem a failing play for a
rival company. The author of Hand C was at-
tached to the Rose and probably to Worcester's
Men **and** Hand D represents one of Henslowe's
dramatists. He is the young John Webster. The
identification is based on characteristics of
Webster's metrics and style--feminine endings,
resolved feet, repetition, compulsive rhetoric,
liberal use of conjunctions, sustained, sensational imagery employed ironically and para-
doxically, aphorism--defined by Sanford Stern-
lich ("**John Webster**'s Imagery and the Webster
Canon," *Jacobean Drama Studies I* [Salzburg: In-
stitut für Englische Sprache und Literatur,
n.d.]: chaps. I and IV). Such tests are the
same as those "by which Shakespeare's hand in
Sir Thomas More is adduced" (p. 455). The original draft of *Sir Thomas More* "reached Tilney's
office in early February, 1603" (p. 469). Although the Essex rebellion was two years dead,
his memory was still alive and Tilney reacted
by inhibiting the play but the playwrights cher-
ished the idea that he could be persuaded to
issue a license by minor modifications which
were carried out mostly by Webster and Dekker
under Heywood's supervision. Elizabeth died in
March, 1603. The playhouses were closed, an
outbreak of plague extended the period of clo-

sure and the play was abandoned. The whole
process of collaborative playwriting may seem
mechanical but the manuscript of *Sir Thomas
More* shows skilled craftsmen at work and may
call for a reassessment of the process. Henslowe's hacks may turn out to have been more
careful than crude.

147 Forker, Charles R. and Joseph Candido. "Wit,
Wisdom and Theatricality in *The Book of Sir
Thomas More*," *Shakespeare Studies*, 13 (1980):
85-104.

Defines the principal theme of *Sir Thomas
More* as the revelation of those unique features
of More's mind and personality which set him
apart from ordinary men. These features are
demonstrated in the play by acting out his wit,
his wisdom and his thespian qualities which lie
at the heart of More's complex personality.
The structure of the play, which is extraordinarily coherent in consideration of the numerous
collaborators, is carefully built around the
revelation of these qualities. The play is organized element by element with the chief objective always in mind. One example is the play-
within-a-play in which More takes the part of
Good Counsel. The play's title is given as *The
Marriage of Wit and Wisdom* but it is actually
Lusty Juventus. It was renamed by the playwrights to serve as a kind of descriptive short-
hand of More's personality. The choice and ex-
ploitation of other incidents in More's life
(e.g., the Lifter-Suresby episode, and the insurrection scene), which permit demonstration of
More's wit, wisdom and flair for the dramatic,
exhibit a continuing awareness of the design of
the play. The structural elements are reflected
in and reinforced by the content. Dramatic
metaphor, More's didacticism, his sense of self,
the conflict between public responsibility and
private value and his Christian humility are employed with considerable effect in demonstrating
the play's theme. The notion that man is but a
plaything of Fortune is implicitly rejected.
Admittedly uneven, the play is marred by defects attributable to haste or failure of in-
spiration and by the need to avoid revealing

the truth of the King's great matter, but the
collaborators strove to produce a drama of
thematic and structural coherence with a considerable degree of success. While not a dramatic
masterpiece, it is the most fascinating and revealing stage biography of its time.

148 Marder, Louis. "Stylometry 'Proves' Entire *Sir
    Thomas More* is All Shakespeare's," *Shake-
    speare Newsletter*, 30:4 (September, 1980):
    29-30.

    Reports findings of a stylometric study of
Sir Thomas More by Thomas Merriam leading to
the conclusion that the entire play is by Shakespeare. Merriam had approached his study with
the expectation that he would find a significant diversion in writing habits corresponding
to the five major contributors. His stylometric
analysis surprisingly showed that only one of
forty-one stylometric tests was divergent, and
that the pattern pointed to Shakespeare as the
sole author. Merriam offers no explanation for
the presence of the palpably different hands in
the *Sir Thomas More* manuscript, leaving that to
the "handwriting experts" (p. 30). Marder tentatively speculates that perhaps the other
writers may have been merely transcribing Shakespeare's foul papers.

149 Urkowitz, Steven. *Shakespeare's Revision of
    King Lear*. Princeton: Princeton University
    Press, 1980. Chap. VI, pp. 129-49.

    Presents evidence, drawn from the manuscript
of *Sir Thomas Moore*, of a practice of revision
by Shakespeare in support of the thesis that
the Folio text of *King Lear* is a revised version
of Shakespeare's own earlier draft exemplified
in the first quarto of 1608.

150 Merriam, Thomas. "Did Shakespeare Write *Sir
    Thomas More?*" *Shakespeare Newsletter*, 31:1
    (February, 1981): 2.

    Summarizes earlier work on the authorship of
Sir Thomas More (see item 148). Stylometric

comparison of that play with *King Lear* confirmed Merriam's earlier conclusion that *Sir Thomas More* exhibited the same habits of composition identified in other Shakespearean plays (*Pericles*, *Titus Andronicus* and *Julius Caesar*). An additional stylometric comparison between *Sir Thomas More* and Munday's *John a Kent and John a Cumber* on the one hand and *Lear*, *Julius Caesar* and *Titus* on the other demonstrates that the compositional habits of *Sir Thomas More* are close to those of the three Shakespearean plays but that those of Munday's play are decidedly not.

151 Metz, G. Harold. "Stylometric Analysis and *Sir Thomas More*," *Shakespeare Newsletter*, 31:1 (February, 1981): 6.

Notes that some of the adverse scholarly criticism of Merriam's findings regarding Shakespeare's participation in *Sir Thomas More* (items 148 and 150) centers on the difficulty of harmonizing the hypothesis of Shakespeare's sole authorship with the presence in the manuscript of the hands of five playwrights, and points out that the earlier studies of some scholars, such as Brooke (item 50), R. W. Chambers (item 105), Nosworthy (item 117), Jenkins (item 124) and Blayney (item 133) have led them to the opinion, sometimes tentative, that perhaps Shakespeare wrote parts of *Sir Thomas More* other than Additions IIc and III.

DATE

152 Collins, D. C. "On the Date of *Sir Thomas More*," *Review of English Studies*, 10:40 (1934): 401-11.

Finds comments on the date of composition of *Sir Thomas More* unsatisfactory because they fail to take into account the political circumstances that would explain Tilney's unusually severe strictures. The dominant idea expressed in the 147 lines of Addition IIc is fear of political chaos and many of the images are astronomical in origin. A series of astrologically alarming events culminating in the conjunction of Saturn and Jupiter in 1603 were already causing comment as early as 1599. The eclipse in 1600 was popularly associated with the rebellion of the Earl of Essex of 8 February 1601. Substantial precautions, including extraordinary military preparations, were taken by the Privy Council immediately thereafter and for some time after Essex was executed to obviate seditious movements among the common people. It was dangerous to play or print any reference to the Essex troubles that might inflame ordinary Londoners, apprentices and "the great number of loose and masterless men about the city" (p. 404). This anxious political situation explains both the changes made in the original draft of the play by the authors, to soften references to the turbulent mob and to eliminate allusions to the Court, especially More's speech to his wife; and Tilney's order to leave out the scenes of the insurrection wholly. A date of 1601 fits

into this background and accommodates the known
play writing activities of Dekker and Heywood.
G. B. Harrison privately suggests this sequence:
Dekker, Heywood and Munday wrote the play in
1601 and offered it to the Admiral's who did
not accept it. Then it was offered to the Chamberlain's who suggested changes, had Shakespeare
touch up one scene, and submitted the play to
Tilney but his requirements were so drastic
that it was dropped. This hypothesis would explain the similarity of *Sir Thomas More* to
Julius Caesar, *Troilus* and *Hamlet* written about
the same time and how Shakespeare came to be
associated with playwrights who usually wrote
for the Admiral's.

153 Eagles, R. L. "The Date and Authorship of the
       MS. Play *Sir Thomas More*," *Notes and Queries*,
       177 (1939): 78.

    Notes a reference in *Sir Thomas More* by
Faulkner to the Brownists and says they were
not well enough known to be the subject of a
popular jest before the beginning of the seventeenth century. Therefore the play must be of
a late date. Because Shakespeare was unlikely
to have taken a hand in a play intended for a
rival company, the writer of Hand D must have
been one of Henslowe's playwrights, perhaps
Drayton or Webster. See items 154 and 155.

154 Crundell, H. W. "The Date and Authorship of
       the MS. Play *Sir Thomas More*," *Notes and
       Queries*, 177 (1939): 120-1.

    In response to Eagles (item 153) points out
that the Brownists had sufficient notoriety to
figure in Nashe's mock *Prognostication* for
1591 which negates Eagles's argument for a late
date. His unsupported authorship conjecture is
unconvincing.

155 Onions, C. T. "Brownists (s.v. 'The Date and
       Authorship of the MS. Play *Sir Thomas More*'),"
       177 (1939): 158.

    Eagles (item 153) overlooked the occurrence
of a reference to the Brownists in Stubbes's

Anatomie of Abuses (1583). There is no reason
why they should not have been the subject of a
popular jest at any time after that date.

156 Shapiro, I. A. "The Significance of a Date,"
     Shakespeare Survey, 8 (1955): 100-5.

Contends that the notation of the date in
the manuscript of Mundy's *John a Kent and John
a Cumber* is neither 1595 nor 1596, as it has
been read, but actually 1590, and prints a convincing facsimile of the notation. Since the
date of *Sir Thomas More*, the manuscript of
which is largely in Mundy's hand, can be set in
consideration of the presumed date of the earlier play, then the original version may have
been written as early as 1591, and the additions in 1593, when the Strange's and Admiral's
Men were temporarily associated together because of the restriction of performances due to
the plague.

157 Wentersdorf, Karl P. "The Date of the Addi-
     tions in *The Booke of Sir Thomas More*,"
     Shakespeare Jahrbuch (West), *1965*: 305-25.

Surveys the attempts to establish a date of
composition for the additions to the manuscript
of *Sir Thomas More* and finds the problem still
unsolved. The additions have been dated from
1592 to as late as 1602. Reviewing the evidence adduced under various headings--paleo-
graphic, content of the play, dramatic subject,
theatrical history, the collaborators and the
significance of the collaboration, Wentersdorf
concludes that the collaborative effort on the
original draft and on the additions took place
at some point while the Admiral's and Strange's
companies were amalgamated and playing together
in 1592-94. There is no external evidence that
Shakespeare was associated with Strange's or
the successor Derby's but he was a payee at
court for the Chamberlain's in December of 1594.
According to Henslowe's *Diary* the Admiral's and
the Chamberlain's acted together at Newington
from June 3 to 13, 1594. Thus June, 1594 is
probably the only time at which he could have

been associated with the Admiral's poets. The
original play was written for the combined Admiral's-Strange's troupe in 1592, but plans for
production were deferred because of the plague.
In the spring of 1594 the play was quickly revised with several writers taking a hand and
submitted to the censor but Tilney refused to
license it; whereupon the play was laid aside
for good.

158 Lake, D. J. "The Date of the *Sir Thomas More*
      Additions by Dekker and Shakespeare," *Notes
      and Queries*, 222 (1977): 114-6.

     Accepts date for original version of *Sir
Thomas More* in the early 1590s but not for the
additions. Dekker (Hand E) uses a few colloquial expressions in his addition which are
rare in his earlier plays but common in the
later ones. This places his addition after
1599, possibly later than 1601. The index of
feminine endings, alexandrines and concluding
half lines in Addition IIc is comparable to
Shakespeare's late plays. The only crowd scene
that matches these verse characteristics is
that in *Coriolanus*. On the stylistic evidence
Shakespeare's and Dekker's additions were written after 1600.

159 Jackson, MacD. P. "Linguistic Evidence for the
      Date of Shakespeare's Addition to *Sir Thomas
      More*," *Notes and Queries*, 223 (1978): 154-6.

     Adduces support from linguistic evidence for
a late date for Addition IIc of *Sir Thomas More*,
now generally agreed to be Shakespeare's.
Building on Waller's detailed study of colloquial forms, especially contractions, in Shakespeare's acknowledged plays (item 274), Jackson
constructs a table showing a steady increase in
such forms in Shakespeare's plays from early to
late, according to Chambers's chronology, with
a clear and substantial increase about 1600.
This is, coincidentally, approximately the same
time that Dekker's writing became substantially
more colloquial as demonstrated by Lake (item
158). Jackson's finding supports Lake's study
in the same paper of the metrical qualities of

Addition IIc and his comparison to Shakespearean metrical characteristics which together indicate a post-1600 date for Shakespeare's contribution to *Sir Thomas More*. Shakespeare is
unlikely to have written Addition IIc before
1600, and may well have written it several
years later.

   See also items 95, 100, 102, 111, 115, 117,
124, 133, 143, 146.

SOURCES

160 Schütt, Marie. "Die Quellen des *Book of Sir Thomas More*," *Englische Studien*, 68 (1933): 209-26.

Reviews individually each original scene and addition in *Sir Thomas More* and traces the source. Hall's *Chronicle*, Foxe's *Book of Martyrs* and five contemporary biographies (Roper's, Harpsfield's, Stapleton's, Ro. Ba.'s and Cresacre More's) are considered potential sources. Schütt identifies a source for most original scenes and additions, the principal sources being Hall and Ro. Ba.'s biography, although she concludes that Foxe and the other biographies, except for Cresacre More's, were used. A few episodes not located in any of the sources are assumed to derive from popular tradition. In general the authors of the serious elements of the play follow the sources fairly closely while more freedom is noted in handling comic themes and the More anecdotes.

161 Wilson, F. P. "Shakespeare's Reading," *Shakespeare Survey*, 3 (1950): 14-21.

Traces the sources both ultimate and proximate of the image of humanity preying on itself employed by Shakespeare in *King Lear*, *Troilus*, *Sir Thomas More* and *Coriolanus*, showing that, if the image is not exactly a commonplace, at least it has a long history. Wilson quotes from a discussion of the image in John Poynet's *A Short Treatise of Politic Power* (1556) who cites Theodoretus, one of the Church Fathers.

TEXT AND EDITIONS

162 Farmer, John S., ed. *The Book of Sir Thomas Moore*. Tudor Facsimile Texts No. 65. Edinburgh and London: by the Editor, 1910. Reprint. New York: AMS, 1970.

The only photographic facsimile of the entire MS. Harleian 7368, *The Booke of Sir Thomas Moore*.
Farmer describes the manuscript and its condition which had deteriorated since the date of Dyce's transcription (1844) and pointed out that scholars will be dependent upon Dyce for readings once legible but hopeless in 1910.

163 Greg, W. W., ed. *The Book of Sir Thomas More*. Malone Society Reprints. Oxford: Oxford University Press, 1911. Reprint. Oxford: Oxford University Press, 1961. Includes "A Supplement to Sir Walter Greg's Edition of *Sir Thomas More*" by Harold Jenkins (item 124).

The text is based on a fresh collation of the *Sir Thomas More* manuscript, employing special lighting to assist in deciphering obscured readings. Some reliance is placed on Dyce's text especially for a limited number of readings which had become irreparably undecipherable or disappeared altogether. Dyce's text however is open to criticism in that it represents neither the original nor the revised text but a confused compromise between the two. There are other faults, such as ignoring marks of omission and 206 defective readings. Brooke's text (item 50), based on Dyce's, is derivative, corrects only six of Dyce's errors and introduces two of his own. His introduction is perfunctory and inaccurate.

Describes the state of the manuscript in meticulous detail and identifies Hands C (playhouse scribe), D (possibly Shakespeare), E (Dekker) and Edmund Tilney, Master of the Revels. The play in its original form (a fair copy in Hand S) was submitted to Tilney who returned it with his strictures. Changes were made but it was clear that the play could not conform to the censor's requirements and was laid aside. The appearance of an actor's name in a stage direction indicates that the play was cast but not that it was acted; nevertheless it does help to set the date which is c. 1592-3.

164 Willoughby, Edwin Eliott. *The Printing of the First Folio of Shakespeare*. Oxford: Oxford University Press, 1932. P. 68.

Compares the punctuation of Addition IIc of *Sir Thomas More* to that of the plays in the First Folio and concludes that Jaggard's compositors liberally added punctuation to the Folio texts. They did not produce anything like a type facsimile of their copy.

165 Pollard, A. W. "Shakespeare's Text." *A Companion to Shakespeare Studies*. Edited by Harley Granville-Barker and G. B. Harrison. Cambridge: Cambridge University Press, 1934. Pp. 263-92.

Provides a useful brief summary of the case for identifying Hand D in *Sir Thomas More* as Shakespeare's including two or three slightly revised opinions (pp. 274-8).

166 Shirley, John, ed. *Sir Thomas More: An Anonymous Play of the Sixteenth Century Ascribed in Part to Shakespeare*. Canterbury: Goulden, n.d. [?1938].

The text is based on W. W. Greg's Malone Society edition of 1911 (item 163).
The Introduction, except for sections on "Sir Thomas More and Canterbury" and "The Rise

and Fall of More," is based on Greg's.

167 Jenkins, Harold. "Readings in the Manuscript of
Sir Thomas More," *Modern Language Review*, 43
(1948): 512-4.

Corrects two misreadings of the manuscript.
Dyce misread the end of l. 658 in which the
Sheriff tells the Clown he will hang for having
set ope the counter gates, saying "you must hang
the foly." This reading was accepted by Brooke
(item 50) and also by Greg in both his Malone
Society Reprint (item 163) and in his edition
of the Ill May Day scenes in *Shakespeare's Hand
in the Play of Sir Thomas More* (item 95). Jenkins demonstrates by reference to analogous *th*
and *ch* spellings elsewhere in the manuscript
that the phrase is "you must hange chefely."
Similarly he shows that l. 722 transcribed
as "such trayterous acts" reads in reality
"such trayterous arts."

168 Bald, R. C., ed. "The 'Shakesperian' Additions
in *The Booke of Sir Thomas More* Addition II,
c," *Shakespeare Survey*, 2 (1949): 62-5. Reprint in item 29.

A diplomatic old-spelling text of the 174
lines of the insurrection scene based primarily
on a reading of MS. Harley 7368 in the British
Library supplemented by readings from the
edition by Dyce (1844) for parts of the manuscript that have become illegible. Corrections
in Hand D, apparently in the course of composition, and in Hand C, and readings taken from
Dyce, are noted.

169 Alexander, Peter, ed. *William Shakespeare:
The Complete Works*. London and Edinburgh:
Collins, 1951. Appendix: "Special Transcript
by Sir Walter Greg of Shakespeare's Contribution to *Sir Thomas More*." Pp. 1345-51.

Text of the 147 lines of the insurrection
scene reproduced in type-facsimile from *Shakespeare's Hand in the Play of Sir Thomas More*
(item 95).
Alexander's Introduction describes the prov-

enance and state of the manuscript and comments
on the difficulties with the censor.

170 Black, Ben Wathen, ed. *"The Book of Sir Thomas
      Moore*: A Critical Edition," *Dissertation
      Abstracts*, 13:6 (1953): 1182.

    Prints a full modernized text of *Sir Thomas
    More* assuming that additions and revisions rep-
    resent the authors' final intention. Introduc-
    tion, notes (chiefly textual) and superseded
    readings are supplied, and the manuscript de-
    scribed.

171 Jenkins, Harold, ed. *Sir Thomas More. Com-
      plete Works*. Edited by C. J. Sisson.
      London: Odhams, 1954.

    The text is based on a fresh collation of
    the *Sir Thomas More* manuscript, which has led
    to one or two new readings, and by reference to
    the texts of Dyce and Greg. Deletions in the
    original draft clearly marked or authorial in
    origin have been made and the additions substi-
    tuted where they exist. Other marks of deletion
    are ignored as is the emendation of the play-
    house scribe (Hand C) in Addition IIc ll. 112-4.
    Jenkins describes *Sir Thomas More* as one of
    a group of 220 plays which are dramatized
    chronicles centered around the career of an
    outstanding figure. More is presented as a
    humorous friend of the people. The play is
    very uneven but the insurrection scenes, even
    apart from the one attributed to Shakespeare,
    exhibit buoyancy and vigor. The story of Ill
    May Day of 1517 was well known but certain pas-
    sages make clear that the play's main source
    is Hall's *Chronicle*. Other incidents are de-
    pendent on Foxe's *Acts and Monuments*, the old
    play *Lusty Juventus* and contemporary biograph-
    ies. Arguments for Shakespeare's authorship of
    the three pages in Hand D rest upon a comparison
    with the handwriting of six authentic signatures,
    correspondences between Hand D and misprints in
    Shakespeare's plays, a few unusual spellings
    and some very striking resemblances with Shake-
    spearean imagery and thought-sequences. The
    evidence is fairly strong and the combination

is accepted as conclusive by most but not all
Shakespearean scholars. The most satisfactory
theory on the date relies on the disturbances
of 1593 and 1595, the reference to the scouring
of Moor Ditch in 1595 and the fact that the
playhouse scribe was with Strange's Men in 1591
but was with the Admiral's in 1598, setting a
date of composition in the middle 1590s. Probably the play was not acted in Elizabethan
times and has only rarely been performed in the
twentieth century. He cites two non-profes-
sional productions of the complete play at
Birkbeck College, London (1922) and at King's
School, Canterbury (1938); and a Third Pro-
gramme broadcast of the Ill May Day scenes on
the BBC in 1948.

172 Wilson, J. Dover. "The New Way with Shakespeare's Texts: an Introduction for Lay
   Readers. III. In Sight of Shakespeare's
   Manuscripts," *Shakespeare Survey*, 9 (1956):
   69-80.

   Recounts in the form of a personal narrative
the events that led up to the recognition of
the importance of the manuscript of *Sir Thomas
More*, the efforts to identify the playwright
who composed Addition IIc, and the genesis of
*Shakespeare's Hand in the Play of Sir Thomas
More* (item 95) that attempted to identify Hand
D as Shakespeare's by bringing to bear evidence
from independent lines of argument--paleograph-
ical, orthographic, linguistic, stylistic and
psychological. Wilson sums up: "We shall
probably never be able to prove that Shakespeare
wrote the Three Pages," but, resting on the
variety of evidence as it does, the case will
probably "never be *dis*proved and is bound to
win acceptance from an ever-widening circle of
scholars" (p. 78).

173 Munro, John, ed. *The London Shakespeare*. London: Eyre & Spottiswoode; and New York: Si-
   mon & Schuster, 1957. 6 vols. *Sir Thomas
   More*, vol. 4, pp. 1255-78.

   Text of Additions IIc and III of *Sir Thomas
More* based on Greg's edition of 1911 (item 163)

with references to the editions of Dyce and
Brooke. Gives a synopsis of the play scene by
scene.

Munro describes in detail the manuscript of
Sir Thomas More and reviews the scholarship to
1931, accepting Greg's summation of the status
of the identification of Hand D as Shakespeare's
as that the case for it is stronger than the case
against it (see item 96). *Sir Thomas More* is
dated in 1593. The play is similar to *Sir John
Oldcastle* and *Thomas Lord Cromwell*, especially
the latter, in the conception of its central
figure and its structural rise and fall. Because of parallels between *Sir Thomas More* and
Cromwell in the hero's dressing a servant in
his own clothes, in talk of execution as a
physic and in reflections on greatness, a question is raised about the attribution of Addition III to Shakespeare.

174 Jackson, MacD. P. "Anthony Mundy and *Sir Thomas More*," *Notes and Queries*, 208 (1963): 96.

Questions Greg's conclusion that Mundy could
not have been the original author of *Sir Thomas
More* on the basis of a transcription error
(*fashis*), which in Greg's opinion an author
transcribing his own work could not possibly
have made. Jackson believes it possible that
the error could have been made in the act of
transcribing and its existence is not an argument against Mundy's original authorship of the
play.

175 Honigmann, E. A. J. *The Stability of Shakespeare's Text*. London: Arnold, 1965.
Pp. 16, 28-9, 40-1, 77, 143.

Traces the development of Greg's opinion
about *Sir Thomas More* 11. 110-4 of Addition IIc.
Greg at first considered the state of these
lines to indicate that Shakespeare had lost
patience in trying to reduce the passage to order (item 163). Later he said that the lines
are clumsy but that he now thought Shakespeare
was not conscious that the passage was confused
(item 95). Honigmann finds it difficult to believe that Shakespeare took seriously patching

a play of average quality originally written by
someone else. The three pages of Addition IIc
at best rise to rhetorical commonplaces while
Addition III comes nearer to the precious life-
blood of poetry. It should not be forgotten
that some of the additions cannot qualify as
free compositions in that they fall back upon
dialog transcribed from the original text. The
addition in Hand D fills in a missing scene and
it is therefore quite possible that Shakespeare
copied some of the 147 lines. Shakespearean
spellings in Addition IIc, especially of names,
suggest that he did not fix on final name forms
before he began writing. In collaboration
Shakespeare apparently worked by scenes and
episodes though E. K. Chambers probably is correct in his opinion that Shakespeare starts
most of the themes in the collaborative plays
(item 2).

176 Clayton, Thomas. *The "Shakespearean" Addition
in the Booke of Sir Thomas Moore: Some Aids
to Scholarly and Critical Shakespearean
Studies. Shakespeare Studies* Monograph
Series 1, edited by J. Leeds Barroll.
Dubuque, Iowa: W. C. Brown, 1969. 119 pp.

Comprises a series of aids for the study of
Sir Thomas More, including general notes, text
of Addition IIc, orthographical indexes (punctuation, speech-prefixes, index verborum) and
modern spelling texts. See item 182.

177 McMillan, Scott. *"The Book of Sir Thomas More:*
a Theatrical View," *Modern Philology*, 68
(1970): 10-24.

Contends that the unsatisfactory state of
the text of *Sir Thomas More* as a literary document does not mean that the text is theatrically
incoherent. Many of the additions, although
perhaps made for other reasons, also serve the
need for changes to facilitate production.
Some of the adjustments, for example the elimination of the part of Sir John Munday, seem to
have as a primary reason the easing of cast requirements. A detailed analysis of the deletions
and the additions demonstrates that the action

of the play has been made coherent although
not without some minor difficulties in exits
and other stage directions. But the text as we
have it has been finished to the point of preparation of actors' parts and the prompt book.
In the course of revision three key interior
scenes in succession are called for in the middle of the play. The most likely stage device
was the use of a booth projecting forward from
the tiring house wall. If it was substantial
it may have served as the platform from which
More addressed the mob and the scaffold on
which he was executed. Thus the essential
elements of his career would be played within
or atop the booth structure, visually organiz-
ing the action with consummate skill no matter
how haphazard the manuscript may be from a literary point of view.

178 Beebe, Richard. "'Fashis' in *The Booke of Sir
     Thomas More*," *Notes and Queries*, 216 (1971):
     452-3.

     Addresses two questions regarding the word
fashis: if Munday was copying another author's
original draft, whose was it? And, is the error
necessarily a copyist's error? An examination
of the manuscript shows that the tilde occurs
twenty-five times to indicate a nasal but never
to abbreviate *-ion*. Hands A and E never use
the tilde, Hands S and B for only one specific
use each, Hand D for two, while Hand C uses it
in three applications. If Munday copied any of
the other writers' work it was probably C (identified as the playhouse reviser). Jackson
(item 174) has shown that Munday both in *Sir
Thomas More* and in the manuscript *John a Kent
and John a Cumber* made a number of errors, some
of the same general nature as *fashis*. The evidence of a single letter in a single word in
Sir Thomas More neither proves nor disproves
anything about the manuscript.

179 Jackson, MacD. P. "A Non-Shakespearian Paral-
     lel to the Comic Mispronunciation of 'Ergo'
     in Hand D of *Sir Thomas More*," *Notes and
     Queries*, 216 (1971): 139.

Notes that R. W. Chambers had searched all of Elizabethan drama from 1580 to 1610 seeking the comic *argo* as it is used in *Sir Thomas More*, finding only two and both were in Shakespearean plays. There is a passage in Middleton's *The Phoenix* at 4.3.16 (Sig. H4 of the 1607 quarto) that includes *argo*. The existence of this parallel does not appreciably weaken the case for Shakespeare's authorship of Addition IIc.

180 Wentersdorf, Karl P. "A Crux in the Putative Shakespearian Addition to *Sir Thomas More*," *English Language Notes*, 10 (1972): 8-10.

Explicates Addition IIc of *Sir Thomas More* 1. 140 (cited from Greg's transcript in item 95) which includes the nonce-word *momtanish*, a version of *mahometanish*, meaning barbarous, applied to the mob's conduct toward the strangers. Shakespeare needed an epithet to sum up the inhuman behavior of the London commoners which would be appropriate dramatically and he syncopated it with due regard for the meter.

181 Evans, G. Blakemore, ed. *Sir Thomas More*. *The Riverside Shakespeare*. Boston: Houghton Mifflin, 1974. Pp. 1683-1700.

The text is based on a firsthand examination of the manuscript of *Sir Thomas More* (limited to Additions IIc and III) with reference to the facsimiles of Farmer (item 162) and Thompson (item 95) and the transcripts of Dyce in his 1844 edition, Brooke (item 50), Greg (item 163) and Bald (item 168). Doubtful readings, readings from Dyce, changes and additions are noted. The type facsimile is faced by a modernized text on the opposite page.

The play was probably originally written for the Admiral's Men who wanted revisions and Tilney required substantial deletions and additional revisions. It is uncertain why or at what point Shakespeare took a hand. Evans says it is clear that he was not originally connected with *Sir Thomas More*. The date is uncertain with a preference for 1590-93 for the original play and 1594-95 for the revisions. The evi-

dence for Shakespeare is paleographic, orthographic, lexical, metrical and political in
nature, a quite remarkable convergence of independent lines of approach. If the 147 lines
are really in Shakespeare's hand the manuscript
is very valuable for the light it sheds on textual cruxes in his acknowledged plays. As a
play *Sir Thomas More* is a negligible chronicle
history and except for the insurrection scene
never rises above competent mediocrity. Of
special interest is the play within a play in
which More takes an extempore role. Reproduces
in photographic facsimile folios 8^r, 8^v and 9^r
of British Library MS. Harley 7368.

182 Howard-Hill, T. H. Rev. art. of *The "Shake-*
spearean" Addition in the Booke of Sir
Thomas Moore: Some Aids to Scholarly and
Critical Shakespearean Studies by Thomas
Clayton, *Computers and the Humanities*, 8
(1974): 338-9.

Describes the present state and origin of
the three pages of *Sir Thomas More* in Hand D
which is probably Shakespeare's. If Addition
IIc is not by Shakespeare it is not by any
other Elizabethan author of whose work evidence
survives. This Addition is of the greatest
value for editing the other plays limited only
by its small extent (147 lines). Clayton (item
176) supplies a plethora for the further study
of the document by specialists in paleography,
linguistics and textual analysis. The monograph represents the most sophisticated application to date of computers to a problem of
Shakespearean interest and supplies an excellent
model for anyone of similar interests.

183 Hays, Michael L. "Watermarks in the Manuscript
of *Sir Thomas More* and a Possible Collation,"
Shakespeare Quarterly, 26 (1975): 66-9.

Analyzes the evidence from watermarks and
chain-lines in an effort to arrive at a collation of the manuscript of *Sir Thomas More*.
The leaves bearing Munday's original text have
a different watermark from those of the paper
on which the additions are written. In the

latter sheets the watermarks vary somewhat and
the chain-lines vary significantly. Hays concludes on the basis of his examination of these
phenomena, especially in folios 6, 7, 8, 9 and
16, that folios 7 and 16 were originally conju-
gate. This reopens the question of whether
Hands C (playhouse bookkeeper) and D (Shakespeare) are of separate authorship. Hays
points out that until Greg's edition (1911)
some scholars thought C and D were the same
hand.

184 Brockbank, Philip, ed. *Coriolanus. New Arden
    Shakespeare*. London: Methuen, 1976.

    Examines the identifying signs of "The Copy"
of *Coriolanus* partially in the light of the
variability of speech-prefixes, unusual spellings, colloquial contractions, minim errors
and punctuation of the *Sir Thomas More* passage
in Hand D, finding many features shared by the
two texts (pp. 3-9). Significant structural
and linguistic qualities are common to the
scenes of popular risings in *2 Henry VI*, *Sir
Thomas More*, *Julius Caesar* and *Coriolanus*, all
offering ironic analogies between fact and
fiction witnessing the elusive intricacy of the
relationship between life and art (pp. 36-9).

185 Dawson, Giles E. "Theobald, *table/babbled* and
    Sir Thomas More," *Times Literary Supplement*,
    22 April 1977, p. 484.

    Finds spellings in *Sir Thomas More* which in-
dicate that, if Hand D is Shakespeare's, and if
the key word in the phrase in *Henry V* 2.3.17
describing Falstaff's death was spelled *babld*,
the initial *b* as formed by Hand D could have
been misread as a *t* and the terminal *d* could
have been misread as an *e*. The compositor thus
read *table* for *babld*. This makes it clear that
Theobald was right in his famous conjectural
emendation and, more important, that the paleographical evidence is the best that has yet
been produced that Shakespeare wrote Hand D.

    See also item 95.

IV
The History of Cardenio

IV. *CARDENIO*

See the items in the section on The Plays
as a Group, most of which comment on
Cardenio. Those that *do not* are items
3, 5, 6, 12, 13, 15, 17, 23, 25, 26, 27,
32, 36, 37, 38, 41, 42, 43, 46, 48, 50,
51, 52, 53, 54.

CRITICISM AND COMMENTARY

186 Castle, Eduard. "Theobald's *Double Falsehood*
     and *The History of Cardenio* by Fletcher and
     Shakespeare," *Archiv für das Studium der
     Neueren Sprachen und Literaturen*, 169 (1936):
     182-99.

   Leans toward acceptance of Moseley's ascription of *Cardenio* to Shakespeare and Fletcher in
   the *Stationers' Register* entry of 9 September
   1653. The play may have been omitted from the
   Shakespeare First Folio because it is a collaboration or because no copy was available as it
   apparently was not for the Beaumont and Fletcher
   First Folio of 1647. Moseley may have published
   the play after the registration in 1653 but his
   stock could have perished in the Great Fire of
   1666. The manuscript, like other manuscripts,
   was somehow preserved. Castle decides with
   Graham (item 197) and against Schevill ("Theobald's *Double Falsehood*," *Modern Philology*, 9
   [1911]: 269-85) that Shelton's *Don Quixote* of
   1612 is the source of both *Cardenio* and *Double
   Falsehood*. The structure and style of *Double
   Falsehood* indicates two playwrights. It is not
   possible to determine who the original author
   was, but it appears that there was a collabor-

ation. The popularity of Beaumont and Fletcher
after the Restoration prompted Theobald to
adapt the play to the "Italian-French" mode re-
quiring extensive rework of Shakespeare's part
but less on the Fletcher scenes.

187 Cadwalader, John. "Theobald's Alleged Shake-
          speare Manuscript," *Modern Language Notes*,
          55 (1940): 108-9.

Prints text of a letter from Theobald to the
Countess of Oxford of 10 December 1727, three
days before the premiere of *Double Falsehood*,
inviting her to attend the performance and en-
closing tickets for twelve box seats. In a
postscript he invites her to read the play in
manuscript if she has a mind to do so. Cadwalader is inclined to think that the manuscript
Theobald alludes to is one of his *Cardenio* manuscripts, but it appears equally possible that
he refers to his own manuscript of *Double
Falsehood*.

188 Harbage, Alfred. "Elizabethan - Restoration
          Palimpsest," *Modern Language Review*, 35
          (1940): 287-319.

Describes the practice, prevalent during the
Restoration, of adapting, with varying degrees
of change, Elizabethan plays for the stage, using *Cardenio* as an example. Moseley's ascription to Shakespeare and Fletcher is fairly credible. *Cardenio* and *Two Noble Kinsmen* may have
been excluded from Shakespeare's First Folio
because they are mainly the work of the lesser
collaborator. Theobald probably obtained Moseley's manuscript of *Cardenio*, adapted it and
published it as *Double Falsehood*. Even his
story of its provenance may have a reasonable
explanation. Lady Mary Davenant may be identified with Theobald's natural daughter of Shakespeare's, and as the widow of Sir William Davenant she could have had a *Cardenio* manuscript.
Theobald may only have elaborated or miscon-
strued common gossip. His credibility is supported by the fact that the early *Cardenio*
records were unknown to him.

189 Bentley, Gerald Eades. *The Jacobean and Caro-*
   line Stage. 7 vols. Oxford: At the Clar-
   endon Press, 1941-68. Vol. 4: 826-7.
   Vol. 5: 1104-5.

   Notes that most competent scholars agree that
   Double Falsehood is an adaptation of an older
   play and that several accept *Cardenio* as the
   original. Some have attempted to identify Massinger's *A Very Woman* with *Cardenio* on the basis
   of characters with similar names, but Moseley
   registered both plays on the same day (9 September 1653) making clear that they were different. Others have thought that Theobald's original was a play by Shirley but Bentley says the
   evidence for that is nil.

190 Muir, Kenneth. "Cardenio," *Etudes Anglaises,*
   11 (1958): 202-9.

   Reprint in revised form in item 20, chap. 8.

191 Muir, Kenneth. "Three Shakespeare Adaptations,"
   Proceedings of the Leeds Philosophical and
   Literary Society, 8 (1959): 233-40.

   Discusses Theobald's adaptation of Shakespeare's *Richard II* and suggests a careful review of the adapted play may throw some light
   on the vexed question of the relationship of
   Double Falsehood to the lost *Cardenio*.

192 Frazier, Harriet C. "Theobald's *The Double*
   Falsehood: A Revision of Shakespeare's
   Cardenio?" *Comparative Drama,* 1 (1967):
   219-33.

   Reprint in revised form in item 196, chap. 4.

193 Frazier, Harriet C. "The Rifling of Beauty's
   Stores: Theobald and Shakespeare," *Neu-*
   philologische Mitteilungen, 69 (1968): 232-
   56.

   Reprint in revised form in item 196, chap. 6.

194 Freehafer, John. "*Cardenio*, by Shakespeare and
   Fletcher," *PMLA*, 84 (1969): 501-13.

   Finds the scholarly consensus on the *Car-
denio-Double Falsehood* authorship question limited to: the original authors of *Cardenio* were
Fletcher and probably Shakespeare; and Moseley's
attribution in his *Stationers' Register* entry
derives from an authentic manuscript. On the
basis of the limited information available
about Theobald's three manuscripts, *Cardenio*
and *Double Falsehood* are both based on the
Shelton translation of *Don Quixote* published in
1612. There is some evidence of diversion between the two which indicates that *Cardenio* was
probably closer to the original, e.g., in the
title listed by Moseley, *The History of Cardenio,*
which is the title of the tale used by Shelton
but not by other translators of *Don Quixote*.
Theobald's account of the Downes manuscript is
plausible. Since it had flaws and interrup-
tions, probably it had been cut and perhaps
adapted for performance, as Theobald says, by
Betterton. Gildon obtained this manuscript at
the sale of Betterton's library. Charles Boyle,
Earl of Orrery, probably obtained it from Gildon with whom he was acquainted, and at Orrery's
death his son, the fifth Earl, put his father's
papers under Theobald's regulation. The provenance of this manuscript is thus: at the re-
opening of the theatres Davenant obtained the
manuscript of *Cardenio* that Moseley had in 1653.
He had Downes prepare an acting version which
was left to his widow, Lady Mary Davenant, who
succeeded him as manager of the Duke's company,
and who may be the prototype of the natural
daughter of Shakespeare's in the stage tradition
noted by Theobald. From Lady Mary it passed to
Betterton who succeeded her as company manager,
then to Gildon and Lord Orrery to Theobald. Of
the other **two** manuscripts Theobald says one is
textually superior indicating that it may have
been Moseley's original or a faithful copy of
it. The omission of *Cardenio* from the Shakespeare and the Beaumont and Fletcher Folios
does not prove anything about authorship.
There were seven Beaumont and Fletcher plays

registered but not printed including two still
extant in manuscript (*The Faithful Friends* and
John Van Olden Barnavelt). The Shakespeare
First Folio excludes *Pericles* and *The Two Noble
Kinsmen*, perhaps because they were collabora-
tive, and *Cardenio* may have been omitted for
the same reason. Theobald did not include *Cardenio* in his edition of Shakespeare because he
accepted the canon as represented by the First
Folio and because he had sold the copyright of
Double Falsehood to John Watts on 31 July 1728.
In the same transaction Watts probably also
obtained Theobald's *Cardenio* manuscripts.
Double Falsehood is printed from Theobald's
acting version which was in turn based on the
Downes playhouse manuscript. Most of the cuts,
some extensive, appear to have been made in the
first half of the play, partly to shorten it,
but probably also, since this is Shakespeare's
part, because the style and vocabulary were
considered old-fashioned. The adaptation of
Cardenio is paralleled in Theobald's version of
Richard II. Internal evidence in *Double Falsehood* indicates Shakespeare's presence on the
basis of parallels, archaisms, studies of metrics, vocabulary, verse and diction, and recognizable Shakespeare themes. Fletcher can be
seen in the style, diction and characterization
and in Fletcherian turns of action. The external evidence is Moseley's ascription to the two
playwrights in the *Stationers' Register* entry,
a reference to Beaumont and Fletcher and Shakespeare by Gildon when writing of *Cardenio*, and
Theobald's reluctant and indirect acknowledge-
ment of Fletcher. Theobald knew of Fletcher's
participation in *Cardenio* either from Gildon or
from the *Stationers' Register*. The date of
composition is established as 1612-13 by the
date of Shelton's *Don Quixote* (1612) and the
latest possible date of first performance, 20
May 1613 [the date of the payment for the court
performance during the preceding Christmas sea-
son]. "Thus, largely on the basis of new evidence, it appears that Theobald did indeed pos-
sess three manuscripts of *Cardenio*; that *Cardenio* was written by Shakespeare and Fletcher;
that it was based on the 1612 Shelton trans-

lation of *Don Quixote*; that *Cardenio* was cut
and perhaps altered during the Restoration
period, then altered by Theobald; that Theobald's
lack of forthrightness in dealing with the authorship of the play resulted from his obligation to support his patron's erroneous belief
that the original play was wholly by Shakespeare
and his desire to protect his reputation as a
Shakespeare scholar; and that Theobald probably
destroyed no manuscripts of *Cardenio*" [which had
passed to Watts with the copyright] (p. 513).

195 Frazier, Harriet C. "Speculation on the Motives
of a Forger," *Neuphilologische Mitteilungen*,
72 (1971): 285-96.

Reprint in revised form in item 196, chap. 7.

196 Frazier, Harriet C. *A Babble of Ancestral
Voices: Shakespeare, Cervantes, and Theobald*. The Hague: Mouton, 1974. 161 pp.

Determines that *Double Falsehood* is a deliberate forgery. It is an attempt by Theobald to
reconstruct *Cardenio* or to write the play that
in his opinion Shakespeare would have written.
Theobald's admiration for Shakespeare, his thorough knowledge of the plays, his desire to assert a connection between Shakespeare and Cervantes, his need to establish a reputation in
Shakespearean studies and his poverty were the
motives behind his action. Theobald somehow
learned of the 1613 performances of *Cardenio* or
Moseley's *Stationers' Register* entry of 1653 at
about the time of Knaplock's reissue in 1725 of
Shelton's translation of *Don Quixote*, which he
knew was the source of *Cardenio*. He was in-
spired to take advantage of the great current
reputations of both Shakespeare and Cervantes.
In this he was successful because *Double Falsehood* ran for ten nights at Drury Lane in December 1727, was well received by the public, and
was revived in 1728, 1740, 1767, 1770 and 1791
in London and in 1793 at Bath. He was granted
a patent on the basis of his edition of the
text issued in 1728. The fact that *Cardenio*
was omitted from his 1733 edition of Shakespeare

indicates he was unwilling further to assert its authenticity. Frazier identifies borrowings in *Double Falsehood* from nine of Shakespeare's plays, especially *Hamlet* which Theobald had studied closely in preparation for his attack on Pope as an editor in *Shakespeare Restored* published in 1726 just before he began to write *Double Falsehood*; as well as from Pichou's *Les Folies de Cardenio* (1629) acted in Paris as late as 1722, Behn's *Amorous Prince* (1671), and Part I of D'Urfey's *Comical History of Don Quixote* (1694), all of which are also based in whole or in part on the Cardenio sequence in *Don Quixote*. She doubts that Theobald ever possessed a seventeenth century manuscript, saying that "though one can never disprove that an early seventeenth century manuscript of *Cardenio* was extant in 1727, I believe the chances that this was the case are impossibly slender" (p. 150). She does believe that Theobald thought that he could write a version of the Cardenio story in true Shakespearean style. The question of Fletcher's participation is not addressed.

See also items 215, 218, 227, 233, 245.

DATE

See items 2, 194, 196, 197.

SOURCES

See items 2, 18, 42, 194, 196, 197.

TEXT AND EDITIONS

197 Graham, Walter, ed. *Double Falsehood*. Western
    Reserve Studies 1:6. Cleveland: Western
    Reserve University, 1920.

    The text is a diplomatic reprint based on
    the first edition of *Double Falsehood* (1728)
    with Introduction (pp. 3-24) but without notes.
    Graham examines evidence and scholarly opin-
    ions in regard to Theobald's possession of *Car-
    denio* manuscripts and decides that although
    there is no proof that he had the manuscripts,
    the negative judgments of critics are not sub-
    stantiated and that Oliphant's view to the ef-
    fect that Theobald may well have had them is
    correct. Graham reviews Bradford's finding
    that there are two hands in the play ("*The
    History of Cardenio* by Mr. Fletcher and Shake-
    speare," *Modern Language Notes*, 25:2 [1910]:
    51-6) and that the linguistic evidence is
    strong for Fletcher's authorship of the latter
    half of *Double Falsehood*. The author of the
    first half is more difficult to identify but a
    metrical analysis indicates to Bradford that it
    is unlikely to be Beaumont or Massinger but
    might be Shakespeare. Graham describes verse
    tests of his own that show different patterns
    in the two parts of *Double Falsehood* and, in
    reliance on assumed collaboration of Shake-
    speare and Fletcher in *Henry VIII* and *Two Noble
    Kinsmen*, traces comparable patterns in the two
    other collaborative plays. This points through
    Double Falsehood to joint authorship of *Car-
    denio*. The playwrights were probably Shake-

speare and Fletcher as the external evidence of the *Stationers' Register* entry indicates. The source of *Double Falsehood* is a version of the Cardenio story as set forth in Shelton's translation of *Don Quixote* (1612) and not the version in Croxall's *Adventures on the Black Mountains* as Rudolph Schevill has contended ("Theobald's *Double Falsehood*," *Modern Philology*, 9 [1911]: 269-85).

198 Schwartzstein, Leonard. "The Text of *The Double Falsehood*," *Notes and Queries*, 199 (1954): 471-2.

Notes five verbal parallels between *Double Falsehood* and passages in *Hamlet*, *Romeo* and *Lucrece* which Schwartzstein believes to be true verbal and situational echoes in *Double Falsehood* rather than echoes of ideas, and assesses them as "deliberate imitation of Shakespeare on the part of someone" unnamed (p. 472).

V
The Two Noble Kinsmen

V. *THE TWO NOBLE KINSMEN*

See the items in the section on The Plays
as a Group, most of which comment on *The Two
Noble Kinsmen*. Those that *do not* are items
13, 15, 17, 23, 48.

CRITICISM AND COMMENTARY

199 Macdonell, A. G. "Chronicles: The Drama," *The
London Mercury*, 17:102 (April, 1928): 696-99.

Includes a review of the Old Vic production
of *The Two Noble Kinsmen* (p. 697). Finds the
production uneven which may be because there
are inequalities in the play. The Jailer's
Daughter goes mad in a beautiful, touching,
Ophelian way. On the other hand the dialog between the kinsmen is so full of nobility of
character and sentiment as to be practically
unintelligible. The outstanding performance
was that of Jean Forbes-Robertson as the Jailer's Daughter. Her heart-rending scenes of
wandering in the woods made a painful contrast
to the scene in which she helps her father with
the prisoners when she is a fresh and gay maid-
en. Ernest Milton made Palamon into a comic
character employing a range of tricks of tone
and voice and a comic red wig. The result
added life to the play: one noble kinsman was
quite enough. See item 206.

200 Hart, Alfred. "Shakespeare and the Vocabulary
of *The Two Noble Kinsmen*," *Review of English
Studies*, 10 (1934): 274-87.

Reprint in revised form in item 5, Chap. 5.

201 Alexander, Peter. *Shakespeare's Life and Art*.
    London: Nisbet, 1939. Reprint. New York:
    New York University Press, 1967. Pp. 220-1.

Summarizes in a brief note his findings on
The Two Noble Kinsmen. The play divides readily
into two parts on metrical grounds, one part
attesting to Fletcher's hand.   It was included
in Beaumont and Fletcher Folio 2 (1679).   However neither the metrical evidence nor the ascription on the title page of the Quarto (1634)
weigh against the significance of its exclusion
from the Shakespeare First Folio.

202 Spencer, Theodore. "*The Two Noble Kinsmen*,"
    Modern Philology, 36 (1939): 255-76. Reprint.
    Theodore Spencer: Selected Essays. Edited by
    Alan C. Purves. New Brunswick: Rutgers Uni-
    versity Press, 1966, No. 14, pp. 220-41; and
    in *The Two Noble Kinsmen*. Edited by Clifford
    Leech. *The Signet Classic Shakespeare*. 3d
    ed., rev., 1977.

Finds the story of *The Two Noble Kinsmen* essentially undramatic as Shakespeare and Fletcher must have realized after they started writing the play. Each strove to solve the problem
in his own way; Fletcher succeeded in attaining
his limited objective but Shakespeare failed to
reach his more demanding goal. Fletcher's parts
are first-rate theater; their contrasts and
conflicts make an immediate and successful impression. The Shakespearean parts are static
and, though with splendor, stiff. They are
slow and dense compared with Fletcher's easy
liquescence; the style and imagery is that of
an old man, noble but fatigued, a poetic success but a dramatic failure. The opening scenes
move slowly like a dramatic pavane. The incantation, tone and order are those of Shakespeare,
but the writing is tired, the muscles slack and
old. Fletcher's writing is that of the easy
lullaby of sentiment. The audience is soothed,
smoothed and softened. The emotional tone is
remote, conveyed by falling rhythms and lines

with feminine endings. But Fletcher fails to
exploit the Shakespearean breadth of vision,
the wider implications of the story. Shakespeare again raises the tone with the prayers
to the gods at the beginning of the last act.
Arcite's prayer to Mars is what could be expected and Emilia's prayer to Diana is emin-
ently appropriate. Palamon's prayer impresses
us not with the power of love but with images
of decay. Shakespeare relied on habitual tones
and habitual rhythms, using the artistry of
long practice. He seems no longer interested
in process or in change, nor in the development
of character. His style is that of an old man,
of an expert in the technique of handling words,
which is a kind of mastery, but is dramatically
stagnant. Spencer accepts the division as "now
generally agreed," assigning to Shakespeare
1.1, .2 and .3; 3.1; and 5.1, .3 and .4, and
"possibly more" (Signet Classic, 3rd ed., rev.,
p. 218).

203 Van Doren, Mark. *Shakespeare*. New York: Holt,
    1939. Pp. 335-6. Numerous reprints.

Finds some lines in *The Two Noble Kinsmen*
charming in their oddity rather than beautiful.
The quaint series of little triumphs grow tire-
some. The two fine heroes talk like one gold-
plated man. The cleverness is senseless, as
Shakespeare never was, and the verse drones.
It is imitation and the identity of the con-
triver does not matter.

204 Spencer, Theodore. "Appearance and Reality in
    Shakespeare's Last Plays," *Modern Philology*,
    39 (1942): 265-74. Reprint. *Theodore Spen-
    cer: Selected Essays*. Edited by Alan C.
    Purves. New Brunswick: Rutgers University
    Press, 1966, No. 16, pp. 282-91.

Shakespeare's last plays, including *The Two
Noble Kinsmen*, present a poetic as distinguished
from philosophic solution to the human question
of the Renaissance: rebirth through spring,
through woman, acceptance of things as they are
because, unlike appearances in tragedy where
good may in reality be evil, appearances in the

romances that seem bad are good. Marina and
Thaisa, thought dead, are alive; Imogen is
faithful; Hermione and Perdita are restored to
Leontes. The prevailing tone may be summed up
in two quotations: *Winter's Tale* 3.2.117 and
Two Noble Kinsmen 5.4.134. The poetic solution
to the problem of man's nature is transfigur-
ation. Spencer points out that the word *bless*
and its derivatives occur in the last five
plays (excluding *The Two Noble Kinsmen*) 72
times or 25% of all usages in less than 15% of
the plays. [There are 18 occurrences in *The
Two Noble Kinsmen* which, if included, would
raise the rate to 30% in 16% of the plays.]

205 Spencer, Theodore. "Shakespeare's Last Plays,"
        Shakespeare and the Nature of Man. New York:
        Macmillan, 1942. Pp. 189-91.

    Defines and evaluates the contributions of
Shakespeare and Fletcher to *The Two Noble Kinsmen*. Shakespeare's part moves slowly, with a
deliberate yet vague grandeur, a remote and
half-exhausted exaltation. Fletcher's part is
an accomplished, suave, sentimental piece of
craftsmanship. His contrasts are managed with
unscrupulous and effective opportunism; there is
no depth, no vision; there are no emotional re-
verberations. Shakespeare's share of the play
exhibits friendship, loyalty and union with the
will of the beneficent gods. The rhythms are
those of acceptance and incantation, the figures are the figures of a pageant or a dream.
There is nothing like this in Fletcher's part;
the emotional tone of his share is that of a
man without experience. At the end of his life
as a dramatist Shakespeare wrote plays that
have a character all their own.

206 Agate, James. *Brief Chronicles: A Survey of
        the Plays of Shakespeare in Actual Perform-
        ance*. London: Cape, 1943. Pp. 153-6.

    The playgoer who takes no interest in find-
ing the hands of the two collaborators will
find little in *The Two Noble Kinsmen*. There
must be a valid reason why the play languished
in oblivion for 300 years. The madness of the

Jailer's Daughter has some pleasantly pathetic
moments; that between the Jailer and the Wooer
is a gem. The two battle speeches have the
harsh, ugly splendor of the late Shakespeare.
The production at the Old Vic (March, 1928) was
charmingly dressed and mounted in good Chaucer-
ian vein and was quite adequately acted. Further acquaintance--say three hundred more
years--"might rate the play higher." See item 199.

207 Armstrong, Edward A. *Shakespeare's Imagination*.
London: Drummond, 1946. 2d ed., rev.
Lincoln: University of Nebraska Press, 1963.
App. B, "Shakespearean Imagery in *The Two
Noble Kinsmen*," pp. 203-17.

Finds three new image clusters in *The Two
Noble Kinsmen* 1.1; 1.2 and 5.1; 3.1, 3.3 and
5.1 and in fourteen canonical plays, particularly *Coriolanus* and the romances. These are in
addition to other clusters identified in the
first edition (such as the *kite-bed* cluster)
and verified by Muir (item 20). One new cluster (in 5.1) is of more than usual interest because it derives from two passages in *The Tempest* (p. 209). Armstrong notes in this instance
and in other *Two Noble Kinsmen* passages "slug-
gishness in image-linking" (p. 209); "the spontaneous fluidity of association seems to be
impeded" (p. 204). He concludes that these are
signs in the play that Shakespeare's creative
talents were failing. Image clusters found in
two places are in portions of the play usually
assigned to Fletcher--the opening song and
scene 3.3. The first cluster consists in the
bridehouse-pie linkage which also occurs in
Merry Wives of Windsor and *Taming of a Shrew*.
The second image cluster is the much more firm-
ly identified *Judas-tree-traitor* theme that is
widely spread through the canon, e.g., *1* and *2
Henry IV*, *King Lear*, *Henry V* and *Macbeth*. The
occurrence of these image clusters may indicate
that Fletcher was working under Shakespeare's
direction; or may be evidence that Shakespeare's
ideas have been modified or interfered with by
somebody else; or perhaps that Shakespeare's
contribution to *The Two Noble Kinsmen* "may have
been greater than is generally accepted" (p. 211).

208 Kökeritz, Helge.   "The Beast-Eating Clown:
     The Two Noble Kinsmen, 3.5.131," *Modern
     Language Notes*, 61 (1946): 532-5.

     Distinguishes between the Clown and the Fool
in *The Two Noble Kinsmen* 3.5.131, identifying
the Fool with the traditional May-festival
Jester and the Clown as a typical country bump-
kin. The Clown is characterized by the term
beast-eating over which editors have repeatedly
stumbled. *Beast* is a variant spelling for
beest, the milk a cow gives immediately after
calving, and the word is still current in
English dialects. In the south counties beest
is regarded as unwholesome or unfit for human
consumption and therefore the epithet is a sneer.

209 Harbage, Alfred. *As They Liked It: An Essay
     on Shakespeare and Morality*. New York: Mac-
     millan, 1947.   Pp. 86, 140, 180, 199.

     Considers the moral implications of *The Two
Noble Kinsmen* to be that of a courtly cult exhibiting the triumph of honor, courage, true
love and generosity.

210 Joseph, Sister Miriam. *Shakespeare's Use of
     the Arts of Language*. New York: Columbia
     University Press, 1947.

     Cites *The Two Noble Kinsmen passim* in sup-
port of the thesis that the extraordinary vitality and richness of Shakespeare's language
is due in part to his knowledge of a current
theory of composition based on grammar, rhetoric and logic. She notes especially the use
of rhetorical figures such as proparalepsis,
metathesis, epergesis, anthimeria, diacope and
many others (pp. 51-3, 57, 62-4, 86-7).   Sister
Miriam also draws attention to individual
Shakespearean linguistic qualities such as in-
ventiveness (pp. 124-5, 133, 146); his use in
argumentation of syllogisms (p. 179); implied
promises and threats (p. 223); and supplication
(pp. 250-1).

211 Vancura, Zdenek. "The Problems of the Shake-
        spearean Canon," *Philologica* 4:2. Supple-
        ment to *Casopisu pro Moderni Filologii*, 32
        (1948): 17-18.

        Reports on the third annual Shakespeare con-
        ference at Stratford-upon-Avon, August 1948,
        concerning *Timon of Athens*, *Pericles*, *Henry VIII*
        and *Two Noble Kinsmen*. Mincoff claimed that
        Shakespeare and Fletcher collaborated on *The
        Two Noble Kinsmen*, but Bethell opposed this view
        and found that Beaumont was most likely to be
        the author. Sisson spoke against the probabil-
        ity of any Shakespearean collaboration. Ellis-
        Fermor argued that on aesthetic evidence the
        play could not possibly be Shakespeare's work.

212 Partridge, A. C. *The Problem of Henry VIII
        Reopened*. Cambridge: Bowes & Bowes, 1949.
        35 pp.

        In the course of a comprehensive review of
        and revalidation of the evidence for the col-
        laboration of Shakespeare and Fletcher in *Henry
        VIII*, with emphasis on grammatical idiom, or-
        thography, syntax and other linguistic habits
        of composition, Partridge offers the opinion
        that *Henry VIII* was included by Heminges and
        Condell in the First Folio based on their
        knowledge of how much of the play Shakespeare
        wrote and that *Two Noble Kinsmen* was excluded
        on their knowledge of the "fact that their col-
        league wrote little of it, if anything at all"
        (p. 34).

213 Pettet, E. C. *Shakespeare and the Romance Tra-
        dition*. London: Staples, 1949. Chap. 7,
        "The 'Romances,'" pp. 161-99.

        Defines the qualities that set *The Two Noble
        Kinsmen* apart from the other Shakespearean ro-
        mances. The substance and spirit of the play
        derive from the oldest layer of romantic tra-
        dition. Its setting is consistently medieval
        and the story is unique among the plays in
        which Shakespeare had a hand for its fidelity
        to the chivalric code. This is to be seen
        throughout the play in such incidents as

Theseus's decision in the first scene to employ
his sword to do a good turn for the grieving
Queens *before* his wedding, a more truly chivalric commitment than in Chaucer's *Knight's Tale*
in which the attack on Thebes occurs after the
wedding; in the frequent striking of the key-
note of honour; in the recognition of Palamon
and Arcite that although they despise their
corrupt uncle King Creon they must fight for
him because they owe a service to Thebes; in
the old favorite conflict of romance--love
against friendship; in the courtesy they re-
ciprocally exhibit in arming each other in
preparation for their fight over Emilia. The
setting reflects the romantic tone of Chaucer's
tale: the castle, the rose garden, the woods,
the May morning and the field of tournament.
However it should be noted that there are differences between *Two Noble Kinsmen* and the
Knight's Tale. In the play there is little
trace of the lugubrious vein of romantic love,
as, for example, Arcite's physical decline from
love-sickness depicted in Chaucer; but the most
important difference is in the heroine. Chaucer's Emilye is a typical lady of the lists who
delights in the tournament for her hand and, as
he says, is a follower of the favor of Fortune.
Shakespeare's Emilia is far more sensitive, will
not be persuaded to witness the deeds of honor
in her name, cannot decide between her two
lovers who are equal in their nobility and does
not want to be the cause of the death of one of
them. All the spirit and motion of the play
are obviously generated from the old chivalric
code and unless the conventions of chivalry are
accepted the plot is absurdly impossible.

214 Harbage, Alfred. *Shakespeare and the Rival
        Traditions*. New York: Macmillan, 1952.
        App. C, "Shakespeare as Expurgator," pp.
        351-8.

    Notes that Shakespeare tends to eliminate
from his plays references to acts of illicit
love found in his sources. In Chaucer's *Knight's
Tale* Palamon in his prayer to Venus vows to war
against chastity. This is not part of the
prayer in *The Two Noble Kinsmen*. It is also

worthy of note that the Jailer's Daughter is disrespectfully used only in those scenes thought to be Fletcher's.

215 Mincoff, M. "The Authorship of *The Two Noble Kinsmen*," *English Studies*, 33 (1952): 97-115.

Assesses the external evidence for collaborative authorship of *The Two Noble Kinsmen* as extraordinarily strong. The attribution to Fletcher and Shakespeare in the entry on the *Stationers' Register* and the repetition on the title page of the quarto by a reliable stationer are of considerable weight. This is the first and only mention in print of a Fletcher-Shakespeare collaboration and is unusual, and therefore convincing, since if the publisher, Waterson, had any doubt about the authorship he could have attributed the play to Beaumont and Fletcher whose plays were then at the height of their popularity. There is evidence that Shakespeare and Fletcher wrote *Henry VIII* and *Cardenio* which substantially supports Waterson's attribution. Against the separate evidentiary weight of the authorship of these three plays, which is significantly reinforcing, there is only one piece of opposing external evidence --it was not admitted to the Shakespeare First Folio. This may be due to a mislaid manuscript, later recovered, or reconstituted as in the case of *Winter's Tale*, or it may have been excluded because Shakespeare's contribution was only about a quarter of the whole whereas in the case of *Henry VIII* it was substantially greater. Much of the adverse criticism of *The Two Noble Kinsmen* is based on a conviction that Shakespeare could not have written some scenes, but critics forget or neglect similar scenes in *All's Well That Ends Well, Cymbeline, Macbeth, King Lear, Romeo and Juliet, Julius Caesar* and *Othello*. The solemn operatic opening, for example, with its atmosphere of deep sorrow complained of as mere verbiage and clap-trap is in fact a stroke of genius preparing for the harsh treatment of the captives (Palamon and Arcite) and the ultimate death of Arcite. The portraiture is perhaps less impressive than Shake-

speare's best but better than that of, for example, *Cymbeline* and its deficiencies are no
argument against Shakespeare's participation.
The style and language is that of the late
Shakespeare and it is surely as absurd to credit
the pedestrian Massinger with the brilliant
poetry of *The Two Noble Kinsmen* as it is in a
different way to compare it to Beaumont's limp-
id clarity of language. The play shows a
thoroughly Shakespearean richness of style.
A comprehensive review of the imagery, especially of Act 1, yields a rich Shakespearean har-
vest. The images are more elaborated than usual
in Shakespeare, but this is characteristic of
his romances. The idea of an epigone imitating
the minutiae of Shakespeare's style and capable
of splendid poetry yet never repeating the attempt is fanciful. In the face of this to dis-
miss Waterson's ascription is ostrich-like. In
all probability his attribution is based on reliable information from the King's Men.

216 Waith, Eugene M. *The Pattern of Tragicomedy in
        Beaumont and Fletcher*. Yale Studies in
        English Vol. 120. New Haven: Yale University
        Press, 1952. Chap. 4, No. 6 "Tragicomedies
        Written in Collaboration," pp. 135-8.

    Argues that the collaborative tragicomedies
of Fletcher, including *The Two Noble Kinsmen*,
exhibit no special characteristics different
from Fletcher's unaided examples of the genre.
Waith finds that Shakespeare's participation,
although it has been questioned, is now generally accepted.

217 Oras, Ants. "'Extra Monosyllables' in *Henry
        VIII* and the Problem of Authorship," *Journal
        of English and Germanic Philology*, 52 (1953):
        198-213.

    Studies the frequency of "extra monosyllables"
forming the last metrically unstressed part of
feminine endings in relation to the total number
of feminine endings to which Alexander called
attention ("Conjectural History, or Shakespeare's
Henry VIII," *Essays and Studies*, 16 [1930]: 85-
120) in an effort to determine whether or not

there are two distinctive hands in *Henry VIII*
and *Two Noble Kinsmen*, employing *Cymbeline*,
Winter's Tale, *Tempest*, *Valentinian*, *Bonduca*
and *Monsieur Thomas* as controls. Oras adjusts
weight accorded statistical evidence by consideration of literary objectives such as a
special stylistic cadence perceived for Caliban.
Three scenes in *Two Noble Kinsmen* (1.4 and .5;
3.2) are excluded from the data because of con-
troversy as to authorship. They would have
little effect on the statistics. Oras's counts
and percentages of extra monosyllables clearly
show a significant diversion of usage in different parts of *Henry VIII* and *Two Noble Kinsmen*, matching the usages in the control plays,
generally along the lines of the traditional
ascription to Shakespeare and Fletcher in the
two collaborations. This is not only true of
the two plays as units but, with a few excep-
tions, also scene by scene. An analysis of the
qualitative characteristics of this prosodic
feature in the two plays demonstrates another
important difference supporting the quantita-
tive difference. Fletcher dwells on the extra
monosyllable and employs repetition, alliteration
and internal rhyme or near-rhyme, seemingly to
draw attention to the device, sometimes to the
detriment of the logical stress; while Shakespeare handles his extra monosyllables so as to
avoid problems of stress, and to facilitate the
smooth flow of the verse. He also clearly
chooses variety rather than repetition and has
few weighted extra monosyllables. This showing
demonstrates the presence of two playwrights in
Henry VIII and *Two Noble Kinsmen*, supports the
contention that Shakespeare and Fletcher are
the collaborators and that the traditional division of the plays between the two is correct.

218 Halliday, F. E. *The Poetry of Shakespeare's
    Plays.* London: Duckworth, 1954. Chap. 7,
    Epilogue *Henry VIII, The Two Noble Kinsmen*,
    pp. 188-93.

Concludes that despite the absence of extern-
al evidence for Fletcher's participation in
Henry VIII, on the model of *Cardenio* and *Two
Noble Kinsmen* it is almost certain that he wrote

half of *Henry VIII*. Halliday discusses division of collaboration and differences in style in *Henry VIII* and finds the pattern repeated in *The Two Noble Kinsmen*. He discerns a sharp contrast in dramaturgy between the partners. Fletcher is responsible for the ridiculous and revolting subplot and rarely rises above the level of a smutty and sentimental mediocrity, while Shakespeare writes some of his noblest poetry and Theseus's final speech is a not inappropriate valediction.

219 Muir, Kenneth. "The Kite Cluster in *The Two Noble Kinsmen*," *Notes and Queries*, 199 (1954): 52-3.

    Announces identification in *The Two Noble Kinsmen* of Armstrong's *kite* cluster (item 207). The substance of this article is reprinted in revised form in item 20, p. 118.

220 *The Dayton Daily News*. "*Two Noble Kinsmen* Well Done at Antioch," 11 August 1955.

    Reviews Antioch Area Theatre production of *The Two Noble Kinsmen* produced and directed by Arthur Lithgow in the Fourth Annual Shakespeare Festival. The production is opulent, the costuming spectacular. The acting is very successful, notably Ellis Rabb as Palamon, Pauline Flanagan as Hippolyta, and Jacqueline Brookes, who, as the Jailer's Daughter, couldn't have been better. The play is rarely performed but it is difficult to see why this is so. The Antioch production has proved that it is well worth doing. The Festival Theatre believes that this production is the first for the play in America. There were eight performances.

221 Hyde, Mary C., comp. "Current Theater Notes." *Shakespeare Quarterly*, 6 (1955): 67-88.

    Lists a classical arena production of *The Two Noble Kinsmen* by the Harvard Dramatic Club, performed alternately with *The Comedy of Errors* April-June 1954, directed by Harold Stones.

222 Jorgensen, Paul A. *Shakespeare's Military
World*. Berkeley: University of California
Press, 1956. Pp. 176-8; 187-8.

Finds that Shakespeare expressed his dramatic
program for the concept of war in Arcite's
prayer to Mars which celebrates the god's splendid, amoral power, and describes war's more
purposeful aspects as a great corrector of enormous times and the "plurisy" of people.

223 Muir, Kenneth. "Shakespeare's Hand in *The Two
Noble Kinsmen*," *Shakespeare Survey*, 11 (1958):
50-9.

Reprint in revised form in item 20, chap. 6.

224 Nicoll, Allardyce. "Shakespeare and the Court
Masque," *Shakespeare Jahrbuch*, 94 (1958):
51-62. Reprint. *Shakespeare's Later Comedies: An Anthology of Modern Criticism*,
edited by D. J. Palmer. Harmondsworth:
Penguin, 1971. Pp. 160-71.

Assesses the influence of the Jacobean court
masque on Shakespeare's plays and concludes that
significant influence is limited to Inigo Jones's
changing scenes which may have given rise to
Prospero's most noteworthy speech in 4.1.151-8
of *The Tempest*. This influence does not necessarily point to a new type of Shakespearean
drama written especially for the Blackfriars.
Only in the case of *The Two Noble Kinsmen* is
there any external evidence that a play of
Shakespeare's was presented at the Blackfriars,
and that is late and therefore doubtful.

225 Griffin, Alice, comp. "Current Theater Notes
1958-1959," *Shakespeare Quarterly*, 11 (1960):
97-115.

Lists production of *The Two Noble Kinsmen*
13-18 June 1959 by the Reading University Drama
Society at the University Open Air Theatre,
Stratford-upon-Avon.

226 Ellis-Fermor, Una. *Shakespeare the Dramatist,
and other papers*. Edited by Kenneth Muir.

London: Methuen; and New York: Barnes and
Noble, 1961. Chap. 10, *"The Two Noble Kinsmen"* pp. 177-86. Read at the 1949 *Shakespeare Survey* Conference.

Discusses the parts of *The Two Noble Kinsmen*
not accepted as Fletcher's. The *Stationers'
Register* entry and the 1634 title-page are too
late to be convincing evidence of Shakespeare's
authorship. Internal aesthetic evidence must
be addressed. Aspects of *Cymbeline*, *Winter's
Tale*, *Henry VIII*, *Pericles* and *Timon* seem like
The Two Noble Kinsmen but evaporate on nearer
inspection. The undeniably Shakespearean tone
is more probably a strong Shakespearean reminiscence. Hart's vocabulary studies do not establish Shakespeare's authorship. The style is
a dazzling imitation of Shakespeare, not Shakespeare himself. Syntax, cadence and imagery
exhibit surprising feats of reproduction but
are quite unlike Shakespeare when dissected.
The shallowness of Emilia, the superficial nov-
elty of Hippolyta, the false motivation, the
evoking of emotion by undramatic methods reveal
habits of thought and technique not like Shakespeare. There is no organic relation of plot
and character or of plot and motive. Tragic in-
evitability does not emerge. The plan of the
play is unlike Shakespeare's known designs in
the underlying thought, in character and plot
and in the nature of its style, the brilliance
of which is startling not illuminating, and in
the absence of interlocking of motive and event.
The author's knowledge of Shakespeare is superb,
going far deeper than mere reminiscence, but it
is not Shakespeare. Increasingly as one reads
the play there is the haunting suggestion of
Beaumont and Fletcher in the part usually
thought to be Shakespearean. The disharmony between the elements of style and the total effect
of the play is a characteristic of *The Two Noble
Kinsmen* but without parallel in Shakespeare's
mature work. The play is least like Shakespeare
in its style which is not strictly dramatic.
Muir notes (p. 186) that in 1957 Ellis-Fermor,
while continuing to deny Shakespeare's part-
authorship, was not as positive as she had been
in 1949.

227 Hoy, Cyrus. "The Shares of Fletcher and his
    Collaborators in the Beaumont and Fletcher
    Canon (VII)," *Studies in Bibliography*, 15
    (1962): 71-90.

Concludes series of seven articles on Fletcherian collaboration with an account of his
presumptive collaborations with Shakespeare
in *Two Noble Kinsmen* and *Henry VIII* [*Cardenio*
is not mentioned]. The ascription on the
title page of the quarto of *The Two Noble Kinsmen* to Fletcher and Shakespeare is supported as
far as Fletcher is concerned by the linguistic
evidence in certain specific scenes and there
is evidence of a collaborator in other scenes,
but the presence of Shakespeare will have to
be established on other than linguistic grounds.
Shakespeare uses no language forms which can
serve to point immediately and unmistakably to
his presence in a play of doubtful authorship.
Sometimes the linguistic practices of the two
playwrights coincide. When the form *'em*, for
example, occurs relatively frequently in a
Shakespeare play (*Timon* and *Antony and Cleopatra*) there is little to distinguish its rate
of usage from that in those plays of Fletcher's
in which it is found least frequently (*Women
Pleased* and *The Mad Lover*). The frequency
of occurrence of such linguistic forms as *'em*,
i'th and *h'as* (he has) is helpful in distinguishing between Shakespeare and Fletcher but
the most effective evidence consists in Shakespeare's use of *hath* and *doth* and in his avoid-
ance of *ye*. *Doth*, for example, occurs three
times in a single one of Fletcher's unaided
plays (*Woman's Prize*), while in Shakespeare's
late plays its use ranges from a low of five
(*Antony*) to a high of thirty-six (*Troilus*).
All thirty-seven *ye's* in the quarto text of *The
Two Noble Kinsmen* are in scenes that exhibit
stylistic characteristics of Fletcher; none
occur in the other scenes. *Hath* is used three
times in scenes that otherwise seem to be Fletcher's, thirteen times in the others. *'Em*
occurs thirty-seven times in Fletcher scenes,
sixteen in the others. On the basis of the
linguistic evidence Hoy divides the play as
follows: Shakespeare: 1; 2.1; 3.1-2; 5.1b

(from exit of Palamon to end), .3 and .4.
Fletcher: 2.2-6; 3.3-6; 4; 5.1a (to exit of
Palamon) and .2.   The attribution to Shakespeare on linguistic grounds is supported by
evidence from style, versification and imagery.

The relatively low incidence of *ye* in the
quarto has been discussed by Waller (item 272).
Hoy concludes that the theory of mixed copy
cannot account for the linguistic evidence,
especially the absence of *ye* in the non-Fletcherian scenes and thinks Waterson's copy was
an intermediate scribal transcript, Waller's
alternative suggestion.

228 Kermode, Frank. *William Shakespeare: The
        Final Plays.* Writers and their Work, No. 155.
        London: Longmans, 1963.

Includes *The Two Noble Kinsmen* in a discussion generally limited to *Pericles*, *Cymbeline*,
Winter's Tale and *Tempest* although he considers
it to be predominantly Fletcher's play. *The
Two Noble Kinsmen* was planned by Fletcher although Shakespeare had a part in it.   It is
best thought of as a play by Fletcher to which
Shakespeare contributed (p. 52).

229 Camden, Carroll.   "On Ophelia's Madness,"
        Shakespeare Quarterly, 15 (1964): 247-55.

Compares madness of Jailer's Daughter in
Two Noble Kinsmen with that of Ophelia (pp.
253-4).   Both suffer from love melancholia and
exhibit similar symptoms.   "The parallel of
Ophelia's madness and that of the Jailer's
Daughter ... is very apt; and it strengthens
the belief that Ophelia is 'distract' from unrequited love" (p. 253).

230 Edwards, Philip.   "On the Design of *The Two
        Noble Kinsmen,*" *Review of English Litera-
        ture*, 5 (1964): 89-105.   Reprint. *The Two
        Noble Kinsmen*.   Edited by Clifford Leech.
        The Signet Classic Shakespeare, 3d ed.,
        rev. 1977.

Argues that the central theme of *The Two
Noble Kinsmen* is the progress from the inno-

cence of spontaneous friendship, such as that
between Theseus and Pirithous, Emilia and
Flavina, and Palamon and Arcite, to the rich
experience of sexual love--that of Theseus and
Hippolyta, of Palamon and Arcite for Emilia
and of the Jailer's Daughter for Palamon. The
growth of experience is not attained without
pain and loss. In *The Two Noble Kinsmen* the
thesis is that the finer relationship of friendship must be sacrificed as part of the unavoid-
able price of progress toward the richer relationship of sexual passion, chiefly as demonstrated in the deterioration of the noble bond
between Palamon and Arcite. Of this loss the
two kinsmen are well aware and comment on it at
several points, most sharply at the end of the
play, first by Arcite after he defeats Palamon
and then by Palamon who gains Emilia only by
reason of the fatal injury to Arcite. The idea
of the play is very carefully set forth in the
first three solemn, slow moving scenes which
Edwards believes are Shakespeare's. The progress from innocence to experience develops
through the whole middle portion of both the
main plot and the subplot, reaching its apogee
in Palamon's prayer to Venus. Shakespeare
planned the play and his grand design sags at
times. These are the points at which Fletcher
takes over, but that he knew the design and
tried his best to fill it out is inescapable.
The central idea is repeatedly approached from
different points and cumulatively built up by
comments and speeches which lie about the hub
of the plots, and which is in turn illuminated
by the reflected light of the surrounding med-
itations. We are given, clearly enough, a life
in two stages: youth in which spontaneous
friendship is dominant, and the riper age of
sexual love. It is a pity that Shakespeare did
not write the whole of the play, but there is
real intellectual substance in the work even as
it is. Edwards assigns 1.1-3; 3.1; and 5.1,
.3 and .4 to Shakespeare, the rest to Fletcher,
but acknowledges that there are some scenes
about which there could be debate.

231 Jones, M. G. "*The Two Noble Kinsmen*." *New
     Theatre Magazine*, 1964 No. 3 (July-

September): 18-9.

Reviews provenance, authorship, date and stage history of *The Two Noble Kinsmen* and notes the production presented in the garden of the Royal Fort, Bristol by the Department of the Drama of the University of Bristol, 14-18 July 1964.

232 Smith, Irwin. *Shakespeare's Blackfriars Playhouse: Its History and Its Design*. New York: New York University Press, 1964. Pp. 213, 218, 234, 236-7, 260, 349, 361, 377-8.

Discusses the staging of *The Two Noble Kinsmen* in connection with the Blackfriars repertory. Smith provides a detailed review of the staging of the prison sequence, 2.1 and .2, and of Emilia's prayer in 5.1.

233 Bertram, Paul. *Shakespeare and The Two Noble Kinsmen*. New Brunswick: Rutgers University Press, 1965. 306 pp.

Contends that the foundations of the original division of authorship of *The Two Noble Kinsmen* by Spalding (1833) and Hickson (1847), generally accepted for over a century, are based on impressionistic judgments rather than objective evidence. Later support for the division from evidence of metrical tests and diction, vocabulary and orthographic studies can be shown to point to distributions different from that generally accepted. Recent commentators such as Muir (item 20) and Waller (item 272) tend to accept as axiom that there is more than one author and then to devote their efforts to identifying the contributions of each. Bertram's stated objective is to examine the evidence afresh. The quarto of 1634 "contains evidence strongly suggestive of one or more authors' hands in the manuscript" (p. 62). Waller's bibliographical evidence and Hoy's (item 227) linguistic evidence for assigning the various scenes to Shakespeare and Fletcher are unpersuasive. A comprehensive assessment

of the quarto text leads to the conclusion that
the printer's copy was an authorial manuscript
and in Shakespeare's hand. A possible reason
for the exclusion of *Two Noble Kinsmen* from the
Shakespeare First Folio is that the manuscript
was temporarily lost as *Winter's Tale* was, but
unlike *Winter's Tale* was not recovered until
some years after 1623. Nor need it be assumed
that the First Folio contains all of Shakespeare's plays since *Troilus* was included only
after apparent copyright difficulties were
solved at the last minute and after Heminges
and Condell seemed to have decided to publish
the book without it. The argument for collaboration in *Two Noble Kinsmen* from analogy of
the divided authorship of *Henry VIII* based on
perceived disunity of design and stylistic differences is frequently cited, but the findings
are in error. *Henry VIII* is entirely Shakespeare's as Foakes in his New Arden edition
demonstrated by adducing evidence of its dramatic integrity and the Shakespearean character
of its design. The belief in the co-authorship
of *Cardenio* is based on four assumptions:

1--Shakespeare and Fletcher collaborated on
Henry VIII and *Two Noble Kinsmen*.

2--*Double Falsehood* was based on *Cardenio*.

3--Shakespeare's but not Fletcher's contribution was almost totally suppressed by Theobald's sweeping revision.

4--Theobald's denial of Fletcher's part in
Cardenio tends to validate the Moseley attribution.

Only one of these assumptions is valid, the link
between *Double Falsehood* and *Cardenio*. The
most reasonable position with respect to the
authorship of *Cardenio* is that Shakespeare had
nothing to do with it. As to *The Two Noble
Kinsmen* the evidence from the use of the main
source, the diction, the structure and some
specific elements points to a single author who
was Shakespeare. The play follows Chaucer's
Knight's Tale closely and in some instances
there are verbal borrowings, most notably at
1.4.28-29, 1.5.13-16 and 4.2.94-95. Close lexical congruence of this type is not characteristic of Fletcher. An analysis of four scenes
from Arcite's triumph in the games to the inter-

ruption by Theseus of his duel with Palamon
demonstrates that the form of the play follows
the *Tale* equally closely. Three of these scenes
(2.5, 3.3 and 3.6) are usually assigned to
Fletcher, the fourth (3.1), interspersed in the
scene sequence, is considered characteristically
Shakespearean. The adaptation of the story
from the source is consistent throughout the
four scenes which have an organic design coherence and linguistic harmony, and do not show
any signs of dislocation. The theories of dual
authorship cannot account for this. The action
of *The Two Noble Kinsmen* falls into three movements: the war against Creon (Act 1); the May
Day contests (Acts 2 and 3); and the final
tournament (Acts 4 and 5). The first two are
relatively simple and straightforward in structure. The third is more elaborate with a heav-
ier mixture of plot and subplot, contrasted
scenes and cross-currents, but it is well con-
trolled and points in its development to a
single guiding hand. No scenes are easily de-
tachable. The frequently criticized close similarity between Palamon and Arcite and Emilia's
indecision are not defects but, on the contrary,
part of the careful control of dramatic suspense.
The prolog presents certain questions. It is
likely that it was composed for the first performance in the autumn of 1613 at Blackfriars
as its opening line indicates. The combination
of the meticulous credit to Chaucer and the
reference to a single "writer" (1. 19) poses a
problem for the dual authorship advocates who
have generally simply ignored it (e.g. Chambers,
item 2). The writer of the prolog could not
have successfully referred to a single author
if the play was collaborative because Blackfriars audiences were knowledgeable and dramatists were public figures in 1613. Thus there
must have been, as the prolog says, only one
playwright. The authorship of the prolog is in
dispute but linguistic and bibliographical
links connect it to the play. *The Two Noble
Kinsmen* was written after 20 February 1613, the
date of the performance of Beaumont's *Masque of
the Inner Temple and Gray's Inn* from which it
borrows in 3.5, and before the allusion in Jonson's *Bartholomew Fair* 4.3 which was first per-

formed on 31 October 1614. Taking the reference to losses in the last line of the prolog
to refer to the Globe fire of 29 June 1613 it
is reasonable to conclude that the play was
written after that date and in time for the
opening of the autumn season at Blackfriars.
The attribution to Shakespeare and Fletcher on
the title-page of the quarto of 1634 is the
only external evidence of Shakespearean collaboration (setting aside the fundamentally
different question of *Sir Thomas More*) and does
not automatically command acceptance. Such
title pages were primarily sales documents and
Fletcher's name was commercially important in
1634. The counter testimony of Leonard Digges,
the stepson of Shakespeare's executor, must be
given at least equal consideration. In a poem
prefaced to an edition of Shakespeare's *Poems*
(1640) Digges asserted:

>   Nor begges he from each witty friend a Scene
>   To peece his Acts with, all that he doth
>   write,
>   Is pure his owne, plot, language exquisite...

Digges's testimony outweighs the authority of
the title-page. That Shakespeare wrote all of
Two Noble Kinsmen is a stable hypothesis. See
item 241.

234 Smith, Hallett. "Shakespeare: Not of an Age,
     but for All Time." *Shakespeare 1964*.
     Edited by Jim W. Corder. Fort Worth: Texas
     Christian University Press, 1965, pp. 101-7.

     Includes *The Two Noble Kinsmen* along with
     Pericles, *Cymbeline*, *Winter's Tale* and *Tempest*
     in a discussion of Shakespeare's accomplishment
     in writing his dramatic romances, which exhibit
     an interesting contrast to the plays that pre-
     ceded them. The reasons suggested for this are
     various and contradictory but two are without
     doubt of prime importance: the change in po-
     litical and social conditions attendant on the
     advent of James I, and the acquisition by the
     King's Men of the Blackfriars Theatre with its
     courtly audience.

235 Seltzer, Daniel. "The Staging of the Last
     Plays," *Later Shakespeare*. Stratford-upon-

Avon Studies 8, edited by John Russell Brown
and Bernard Harris.   London: Arnold, 1966,
pp. 127-65.

Analyzes staging of the last plays including
The Two Noble Kinsmen under six headings:
stage business, facial expression, voice, block-
ing, address, and spectacle and music, based on
the content of the stage directions and comments
in the text.   The staging of these plays exhibits normal development from that of the plays
which immediately preceded.   There is, for example, a continuation of the trend away from
the dramatic soliloquy evident since *King Lear*
which is a natural development of an art.
There is no evidence of a radical departure in
technique from earlier staging as a consequence
of the acquisition of Blackfriars.   Some relatively minor modifications undoubtedly occurred
because of the shallower platform and intimate
surroundings, leading perhaps to a more realis-
tic style of acting.

236 Cutts, John P.   "Shakespeare's Song and Masque
      Hand in *The Two Noble Kinsmen*," *English
      Miscellany*, 18 (1967): 55-85.

Finds scholars generally agree on the broad
distribution between the two collaborators in
The Two Noble Kinsmen.   There are however some
disagreements on the authorship of some scenes
and portions of other scenes.   The results of a
study of masque, music and song elements in the
play can be applied to the solution of these
questions.   Beginning from about 1608 the King's
Men's plays included elements of court masques,
perhaps developing in part from the practice of
having players dance the antimasques at Court.
Robert Johnson, the King's Men's composer,
supplied the music for the dances on at least
one occasion.   Of twenty-seven new plays from
Pericles (c. 1608) to *More Dissemblers Besides
Women* (c. 1615) twenty-two contain masques or
masque-like action.   In *Two Noble Kinsmen* there
are elements derived from the masque (the opening procession, the three ceremonial entrances
of the three Queens, the supplications in the
temple) as well as the morris dance adapted

from Beaumont's antimasque. The wedding procession parallels similar action in *A Midsummer
Night's Dream* and *Henry VIII* but is unlike parallel elements in *Philaster* and *The Maid's
Tragedy*. Throughout the main action of the
play there is unity of song and masque design.
The opening song has a reflection in the funeral solemnity (1.5). Flower symbolism is pervasive and is Shakespearean in tone, matching
particularly the tone of the romances. Color
symbolism is employed to distinguish Arcite
(black) from Palamon (red and white) since the
plot requires them to be equally noble. A rid-
dling quality is present throughout the main
plot of *The Two Noble Kinsmen*. The theme is
set at the very beginning of Act 1 with the
conjunction of the happiness of a wedding with
the grief of the three Queens. It is repeated
again and again in, for example, the happiness
of Palamon and Arcite though in prison, Emilia's
difficult choice, the Delphic responses of the
gods and the paradox of the ending--the winner
loses and the loser wins. Cutts concludes that
the main plot is thoroughly in tune with the
techniques and philosophy of Shakespeare's romances and he inclines to ascribe the whole of
that action to Shakespeare. The subplot is not
discussed.

237 Edwards, Philip, ed. "*The Masque of the Inner
    Temple and Gray's Inn* (1613)," *A Book of
    Masques in Honour of Allardyce Nicoll*.
    Edited by T. J. B. Spencer and Stanley Wells.
    Cambridge: Cambridge University Press, 1967.
    Reprints. Cambridge: Cambridge University
    Press, 1970, 1980, pp. 125-48. The second
    anti-masque, pp. 138-9.

    Prints the text of the masque performed at
Whitehall on 20 February 1613, including the
second anti-masque which was later incorporated
into 3.5 of *The Two Noble Kinsmen*, and the in-
formative commentary by means of which we know
that the second anti-masque was danced by actors, probably some of the King's Men. The
commentary notes that the second anti-masque
was exceptionally well received, and that King
James called for it to be repeated at the end.

238 Rabkin, Norman. *Shakespeare and the Common
        Understanding*. New York: Free Press, 1967.

    Observes that in spite of the existence of
later Shakespearean plays, *The Tempest* does
seem to represent a complete fulfillment of
Shakespeare's career. It is worthy of note
that when he returned to his art in *The Two
Noble Kinsmen* he manifests a strange new de-
tachment. There is little in it of the Shakespeare of the last phase. He seems to have
submerged his personality in an effort to manu-
facture a play conforming to the empty symmetry
of Fletcherian tragicomedy. Rabkin finds persuasive Bertram's case for sole Shakespeare
authorship (item 233).

239 Smith, Hallett. "Shakespeare's Last Plays:
        Facts and Problems," *Shakespearean Research
        Opportunities*, 3 (1967):   9-16.

    Cites Kittredge's statement (item 270) that
there is substantial agreement on the collaboration question but points out that in some
areas of the play scholars are not agreed, some
finding Shakespeare touched up by Fletcher,
others *vice versa* and yet others conclude it is
Fletcher writing under Shakespeare's influence.
Bertram (item 233) has reopened the authorship
question. Criticism of the last plays has followed two patterns: the myth-symbol-ritual-
allegory and that of theology. Neither has
been satisfactory, both resulting in distortion.
Accepts date of autumn, 1613 for composition of
The Two Noble Kinsmen.

240 Edwards, Philip. *Shakespeare and the Confines
        of Art*. London: Methuen, 1968.

    Includes a summary version of item 230.

241 Hoy, Cyrus. Rev. art. of *Shakespeare and The
        Two Noble Kinsmen* by Paul Bertram (item 233).
        Modern Philology, 67 (1969): 83-8.

    Disputes Bertram's thesis that Shakespeare
is the sole author of *The Two Noble Kinsmen*.
The argument that there is but one voice to be

heard in the play cannot prevail against the
accumulated metrical, linguistic and bibliographical evidence that identifies certain qualities, chiefly syntactical and rhetorical, of
Fletcher's writing that are evident in the play.
The spellings that Bertram says are Shakespearean are common in the writing of Ralph Crane,
the scribe employed by the King's Men, and the
misprints that he says point to Shakespearean
foul papers are incidental to the Elizabethan
Secretary hand generally. The recognized dislocation between 2.1 and 2.2 which scholars
have taken as evidence of a defect of joinery
between the work of the two playwrights Bertram
would explain away by moving 2.2 from the gal-
lery to the platform, but this will not work
because it calls for Emilia and her maid to be
at the front of the stage later in the scene
between Palamon and Arcite and the audience.
Bertram's argument that Fletcher was not available to collaborate on *The Two Noble Kinsmen*
because he was working with Daborne, Field and
Massinger on another play during the summer of
1613 is contradicted by the simple fact of
other simultaneous collaborations in Fletcher's
career. The structural unity of *The Two Noble
Kinsmen* does not argue against Fletcher's collaboration because he was accustomed to joint
creation of design with Beaumont, as in *Philaster* and *A King and No King*, which also exhibit a firm structure. Leonard Digges's verses
cannot be taken as conclusive evidence that
Shakespeare never collaborated.

242 Spencer, Christopher. "*Macbeth* and Davenant's
    The Rivals," *Shakespeare Quarterly*, 20
    (1969): 225-9.

    Analyzes Davenant's adaptations of *Macbeth*
    and *The Two Noble Kinsmen* (*The Rivals*) and
    compares the handling by Davenant of his source
    play in each case. He identifies echoes of the
    altered *Macbeth* in *The Two Noble Kinsmen*, thus
    providing an insight into an early Restoration
    adapter's attitude toward Shakespeare.

243 Leyris, Pierre. "La chant du cygne de Shake-
    speare," *La Nouvelle Revue Francaise*, 215

(1 November 1970): 44-57.

Reviews the scholarship on the authorship of
The Two Noble Kinsmen from Pope to 1970 with
emphasis on the opinions of Swinburne, De Quincey, Brooke (item 50), Eliot and Leech (item
273). He analyzes the evidence from style and
concludes that the hand of Shakespeare is unmistakable. Comparing the structural characteristics of *The Two Noble Kinsmen* with those of
The Two Gentlemen of Verona, he finds them similar. Explicit reminiscences of Shakespeare's
plays may point to Fletcher, but the signs of
Shakespeare are general throughout the play,
as in, for example, the similarities in the
Jailer's Daughter's derangement to Ophelia's
and the reminiscences in *Two Noble Kinsmen* of
the doctor in *Macbeth*. The last act is manifestly by Shakespeare, although it is unchar-
acteristically static and shows signs that the
playwright was weary, old and withdrawn. It is
a play that makes considerable demands on the
audience. Although genuine Shakespeare, it is
Shakespeare as an old man who does not speak to
us without revealing his personal cares--for
the last time.

244 Bradbrook, M. C. "Shakespeare the Jacobean
      Dramatist," *A New Companion to Shakespeare
      Studies*. Edited by Kenneth Muir and S.
      Schoenbaum. Cambridge: At the University
      Press, 1971. Pp. 152-6.

      Finds Shakespeare's final plays, including
      The Two Noble Kinsmen, related to both the
      masque and to the older emblematic stages of
      his youth. Bradbrook notes elements common to
      both traditions such as sumptuous display,
      tragicomic violence, horror and turbulence,
      frequently combined in enigmatic or puzzling
      ways and concludes that Shakespeare is delib-
      erately attempting an experimental integration
      of old and new stage conventions.

245 Ure, Peter. "Shakespeare and the Drama of his
      Time," *A New Companion to Shakespeare Stud-
      ies*. Edited by Kenneth Muir and S. Schoen-
      baum. Cambridge: At the University Press,

1971. Pp. 211-21.

Discusses, in a section of his essay entitled
"Fletcher and the Last Plays" (pp. 218-20), the
reciprocal influences of Shakespeare and Fletcher in the plays written for performance at
Blackfriars. Current theories that *Henry VIII*
and *The Two Noble Kinsmen* are Shakespeare's unaided work are exceptionally improbable, and no
doubt *Cardenio* was also a collaboration. Shakespeare would not have refused to learn from
Fletcher but he had known *Mucedorus* and *The
Rare Triumphs of Love and Fortune*, old plays
whose traces are found in his romances, and he
had written *Pericles* before the advent of Fletcher to the stage. Tragicomedy persisted on
the Elizabethan stage from the time of Richard
Edwardes's *Damon and Pithias* (1565). Shakespeare never adopted the Fletcherian stigma--a
mawkish intensity of tone and language--but
kept his toughly obscure late style. The last
plays have a solemnity and splendor of imagination that outpaces Fletcher beyond any reck-
oning.

246 Auden, W. H. Introduction to *The Sonnets*. *The
      Complete Signet Classic Shakespeare*. Edited
      by Sylvan Barnet. New York: Harcourt Brace
      Jovanovich, 1972. Pp. 1722-9.

Notes that Palamon's prayer to Venus is part
of what may have been Shakespeare's last play;
that it is remarkable in its choice of examples
of the power of the goddess. They are nearly
all humiliating, horrid, or express intense
disgust at masculine sexual vanity (p. 1728).

247 Hartwig, Joan. *Shakespeare's Tragicomic
      Vision*. Baton Rouge: Louisiana State Uni-
      versity Press, 1972. Appendix B: "The Re-
      lationship of *Henry VIII* and *The Two Noble
      Kinsmen* to the Tragicomedies," pp. 184-9.

Argues that *The Two Noble Kinsmen* departs
from the tragicomic pattern of *Pericles*, *Cymbeline*, *Winter's Tale* and *Tempest*. The deriv-
ation of *Two Noble Kinsmen* from Chaucer's ro-

mantic *Knight's Tale* and some of the dramatic
qualities particularly of the subplot of the
Jailer's Daughter ally it with the earlier
tragicomedies but it exhibits a fundamental
difference from them in its sunny beginning and
its tragic ending in Arcite's death, the re-
verse of the earlier plays. Joy seems to have
lost in this play the climactic place it had in
the four earlier tragicomedies and in *Henry VIII*.

248 Smith, Hallett. *Shakespeare Romances: A Study
      of Some Ways of the Imagination*. San Marino:
      Huntington Library, 1972. Pp. 33-5.

      Compares the innocence of Marina in *The Tem-
pest* and of Polixenes and Leontes in *The Winter's Tale* with that displayed by Palamon and
Arcite in the second scene of *The Two Noble
Kinsmen*, but finds that that of the noble cousins, in the event, turns out to be different
when they experience sexual attraction. At
this point the theme of pastoral innocence is
transferred to Emilia.

249 Bates, Merete. "*Two Noble Kinsmen* at York
      Theatre Royal," *Manchester Guardian*, 5 July
      1973.

      Reviews the York Theatre Royal presentation
of *The Two Noble Kinsmen* produced by Mervyn
Willis and adapted for production by Richard
Digby Day. Bates finds the performance gay,
sweeping and exuberantly romantic. The play is
acted on a white thrust platform and giant
white balloons float in the central space, gen-
erating excitement. In spite of the promise of
the setting the action drags, but only slightly.
The director and company fight to keep it fresh,
passionate and unexpected. The acting is uneven although the kinsmen played by Malcolm
Armstrong (Arcite) and Philip Bowen (Palamon)
are superbly compelling. See item 250.

250 *The Stage and Television Today*. "Impressive
      Noble Kinsmen," 12 July 1973.

      Mervyn Willis's production at the York Thea-
tre Royal of Richard Digby Day's adaptation of

The Two Noble Kinsmen is an impressive event.
The set designed by Kit Surrey and dramatically
lighted by Colin Black--a white stage with
white backdrop and enormous white balloons--is
striking and highly effective. The two noble
kinsmen are excellently played by Malcolm Armstrong and Philip Bowen to bring out the humor
of their rivalry. Jane Casson plays Hippolyta
with dignity and grace and Jean Viner's Jailer's
Daughter has vitality and pathos. There is no
doubt that the play provides good entertainment.
See item 249.

251 Wickham, Glynne. "From Tragedy to Tragi-Comedy:
      King Lear as Prologue," *Shakespeare Survey*,
      26 (1973): 33-48.

      Shakespeare's late plays were inspired in
   different ways by the accession of James and by
   the early events of his reign such as the Gun-
   powder Plot and the untimely death of Henry
   Prince of Wales on the eve of his sister's wedding. *The Two Noble Kinsmen* "in equal scale
   weighing delight and dole" (p. 47) is a mirror
   image of that most unhappy conjunction.

252 Muir, Kenneth. "Theophanies in the Last Plays,"
      *Shakespeare's Last Plays: Essays in Honor
      of Charles Crow*. Edited by Richard T.
      Tobias and Paul G. Zalbrod. Athens, Ohio:
      Ohio University Press, 1974, pp. 32-43.

      Describes the distinctive qualities of the
   prayers of Arcite, Palamon and Emilia to Mars,
   Venus and Diana in *The Two Noble Kinsmen* and
   compares them to theophanies in Shakespeare's
   other late plays. There are similarities, most
   important of which are common themes and the
   function of such prayers employed by the dramatist as a means of exhibiting the workings of
   divine providence.

253 Petronella, Vincent F. "Stylistic Logic in
      Shakespeare's Part of *The Two Noble Kinsmen*,"
      The Humanities Association Review, 25 (1974):
      38-40.

Draws attention to Shakespeare's use of syl-
logistic structure as an element of style in
Othello, *Hamlet* and *Troilus*. In *The Two Noble
Kinsmen* the same type of stylistic logic is
found in three scenes (1.1; 5.1 and 5.4) which
establish a solid structural frame for the dra-
matic plot. In 1.1 Emilia tells Theseus that
if he does not accede to the request of the
three Queens she will never marry. Since he
does agree to the request, Emilia, in spite of
her reservations, must marry. In 5.1 she prays
to Diana that she, a virgin flower, may grow un-
plucked, but the rose falls from the rose-tree
on the altar, so Emilia must be plucked. The
concluding scene presents a paradox--the con-
quered kinsman triumphs, the victor loses--but
it is logically necessary and an explicit example of the exclusive disjunctive argument,
permitting coexistence of the rational and non-
rational (romantic) elements of the plot.

254 Trewin, J. C. [Review of a production of *The
        Two Noble Kinsmen*], *The Illustrated London
        News*, 262: 6915 (October 1974): 107.

Finds much to admire in an open-air Regent's
Park production of *Two Noble Kinsmen* by the
New Shakespeare Company. The entrance of the
three mourning queens challenges any disbelief
in the ascription to Shakespeare.

255 Clements, Robert Morrison, Jr. "A New Look at
        The Two Noble Kinsmen," *Dissertation Ab-
        stracts International*, 35A:11 (1975): 7251A.

Examines *The Two Noble Kinsmen* and its history from four points of view: the reputation
of the play; comparison with Fletcherian tragi-
comedy; its place in literary tradition; and
masque elements and masque-like scenic effects.
In its opening procession and the funeral march
in the first act, in its use of Beaumont's anti-
masque and in the prayers to the gods in Act 5,
The Two Noble Kinsmen is an exhibition of current stage practice in adapting the masque to
public performance.

256 Rabkin, Norman. "Problems in the Study of Collaboration," *Research Opportunities in Renaissance Drama*, 19 (1976): 7-13.

Finds that collaboration submerges brilliance as it does idiosyncrasy. Shakespeare
found it appropriate in *The Two Noble Kinsmen*
to submit to a Fletcherian decorum (p. 12).

257 Brownlow, F. W. *Two Shakespearean Sequences*.
London: Macmillan; and Pittsburgh: Univer-
sity of Pittsburgh Press, 1977. Chap. 12,
"*The Two Noble Kinsmen*," pp. 202-15; and
Chap. 13, "Conclusion: *Timon of Athens*,"
pp. 216-22.

Defines the theme of *The Two Noble Kinsmen*
as the conflict of Venus and Mars, or in current jargon, sex and aggression. Shakespeare
has however, in contrast to Chaucer, suppressed
the discord and made the rule of each deity a
thread in the weft of Providence. The dramaturgy is not new but what is new is the attitude
of coolly reflective objectivity, making the
play in the undoubtedly Shakespearean parts
stern and rather dark. Palamon and Arcite are
ruled by different appetites and *The Two Noble
Kinsmen* is designed so that neither is preferred. The fascination of the story is that
there cannot be a perfect solution for either
hero. Shakespeare compresses the *Knight's Tale*
and heightens the general contrast; for example,
Thebes is depicted as the city of incontinence,
but in Athens appetite is ruled by reason. The
story presents a difficulty as drama because it
lacks a true "middle" which Shakespeare, whose
design it is, fills by inventing the subplot of
the Jailer's Daughter. The great scenes of Act
5 are Shakespeare's, the scene of the three
prayers splendidly realizing in Mars, Venus and
Diana the sources of the motives in the play,
depicting with poetic and visual power the conflicting forces that must be defined. Theseus
is portrayed as an absolute ruler who displays
qualities of urbanity and tolerance and speaks
with melancholy because he realizes the limita-
tions upon human potentiality. The final im-

pressions are of civility and graciousness, of
irregularity tamed by ceremony and justice, of
Providence acknowledged and the gods subdued to
the order of a large design. *The Two Noble
Kinsmen* is Shakespeare's last datable play. It
may have been a collaboration, but if so Fletcher's contribution follows Shakespeare's plan.
The play is not a valedictory. It reveals an
artistic intelligence in complete control of
its material, and exhibits no sign of dissolu-
tion. It is a drama of ideas, as are the other
romances which naturally developed from Shakespeare's tragedies.

258 Bradbrook, M. C. *Shakespeare: The Poet in
     his World*. New York: Columbia University
     Press, 1978. Pp. 224-5, 227, 234-6.

   Sums up Shakespeare's final days in "The end
of the revels" (chap. 12): the revelation of a
great power breaking up, at its most painful in
The Two Noble Kinsmen, which was probably Shakespeare's last work and in which he returned to
Chaucer, his nearest kinsman in English poetry.
The first scene is an elegy which reflects the
real-life crossing of the death and funeral of
Prince Henry (November, 1612) with the post-
poned wedding of his sister Princess Elizabeth.
Bradbrook restates the substance of her theory
(see item 43) that the play was hastily written
around the unusually successful anti-masque in
Beaumont's *Masque of the Inner Temple and Gray's
Inn*.

259 Frye, Northrop. "Romance as Masque," *Shake-
     speare's Romances Reconsidered*. Edited by
     Carol McGinnis Kay and Henry E. Jacobs.
     Lincoln: University of Nebraska Press, 1978,
     pp. 11-39.

   Examines Shakespearean romance in the light
of New Comedy and the masque. *The Two Noble
Kinsmen* is characterized by ritual (e.g.:
Theseus's wedding) and counter-ritual (the
mourning queens) and a world of illusion suggestive of the masque. The action of the play
is dominated by Venus, not the laughter-loving
Aphrodite, but a menacing goddess.

260 Thompson, Ann. *Shakespeare's Chaucer: A Study in Literary Origins*. Liverpool English Texts and Studies, edited by Philip Edwards. Liverpool: Liverpool University Press; New York: Harper and Row, 1978. Chap. 5, "*The Two Noble Kinsmen*," pp. 166-215.

Finds *The Two Noble Kinsmen* a free adaptation of Chaucer's *Knight's Tale* with a notable change of tone. Where Chaucer was ironic and mocking the authors of the play treat the story seriously. Detailed study of the uses made of the source demonstrates that the following parts are Shakespeare's: 1; 3.1 and .2; 5.1, .3 and .4; and probably 2.1 and 4.3. Since Chaucer's tale does not readily lend itself to dramatization the authors compressed the time-scheme, tightened the structure, heightened the characterization, added a sub-plot and inserted a morris dance borrowed from an anti-masque by Beaumont. The prolog is unusual in its tribute to Chaucer, only one other (non-Shakespearean) instance of this kind being extant. In a scene-by-scene analysis Thompson notes differences in various parts of the play in source adaptation, allusions to the gods and Fortune, handling of the sub-plot, the quality of the verse and other matters that point to a collaboration. She concludes that the individual differences stem from a fundamental divergence of objectives: Shakespeare was writing a romance while Fletcher was writing a tragicomedy. Fletcher's part of *The Two Noble Kinsmen* is less successful than Shakespeare's, perhaps because the story was not of his choice.

261 Howard, Tony, comp. "Census of Renaissance Drama Productions." *Research Opportunities in Renaissance Drama*, 22 (1979): 73-85. "Fletcher and Shakespeare," *The Two Noble Kinsmen*, Cherub Company, 21 November - 8 December 1979, Young Vic Studio, London, p. 75.

This small-scale touring production was hobbled by poverty, inexperience and its all-male cast. The playing of the female parts seemed a sly anti-feminine joke, but the performances of Palamon and Arcite were forceful, sober,

even noble. Substantial cuts in Acts 2 and 3
imparted a sense of consistency which gripped
the audience. The arming scene was most striking. The speaking was musical but, in the
denser Shakespearean passages, incomprehensible;
the grander rhetoric was drowned by percussion.
Striving for effect marred the close. See item
264.

262 Shirley, Frances A. *Swearing and Perjury in
      Shakespeare's Plays.* London: Allen & Unwin,
      1979, pp. 149-50.

Finds few oaths in *The Two Noble Kinsmen* in
spite of the possibilities, considering the
nature of the story, to swear by the old gods.
Theseus on two different occasions swears by
the helm of Mars and by Castor but the most in-
teresting oaths are Palamon's "by this air" and
Cecily's "by wine and bread." Although Mars
and Venus are invoked the feeling of the play
is courtly and medieval and reflects little of
pagan Greece.

263 Andreas, James. "From Festivity to Spectacle:
      The *Canterbury Tales, Fragment I* and *A Mid-
      summer Night's Dream.*" *The Upstart Crow*, 3
      (Fall, 1980): 19-28.

Compares the interplay of serious and comic
materials in Chaucer, primarily in the sequence
of the *Knight's Tale* and the subsequent tales
of the Miller and the Reeve, with that in *A
Midsummer Night's Dream* and (less extensively)
in *The Two Noble Kinsmen.* Shakespeare retains
Chaucer's parodic tendencies but he circum-
scribes comic incidents as plays within plays
or inserts them as incidents of relief in the
more serious dramatic action. Andreas contrasts
the two views of Theseus in Shakespeare's two
plays and his interaction with the comic element, and notes that in *The Two Noble Kinsmen*
he is a sterner character. He concludes that
Shakespeare in *The Two Noble Kinsmen* apparently
loses interest in comic counterpoint while
Fletcher provides what comic element there is
in the morris dance sequence.

264 Berkowitz, Gerald M. "Shakespeare in Edin-
     burgh." *Shakespeare Quarterly*, 31 (1980):
     165-6.

        Reviews the Cherub Company production of *The
     Two Noble Kinsmen* at the New Chaplaincy Centre,
     Edinburgh in the 1979 Edinburgh International
     Festival, 27 August - 8 September 1979. The
     play was presented by an all-male cast in a
     heavily cut but lucid and frequently exciting
     production. Notable were effective differen-
     tiation between Palamon and Arcite and ironic
     parallels between the first and last scenes.
     See item 261.

265 Stoddard, Joseph H. and Lillian Wilds. "Shake-
     speare in Southern California and Visalia."
     Shakespeare Quarterly, 31 (1980): 254; 258-9.

        Reviews the Globe Playhouse of Los Angeles
     production of *The Two Noble Kinsmen* by the
     Shakespeare Society of America 27 June - 14 July
     1979. The reviewers found the romance reward-
     ing for its value as audience entertainment
     which shone with unexpected brilliance among the
     canonical plays. This *Two Noble Kinsmen* was
     director Walter Scholz's fifth presentation for
     the Globe and his best, winning Los Angeles
     Drama Critics Awards for the production and for
     Suzanne Peters's performance as the Jailer's
     Daughter. The production enabled founder and
     executive producer R. Thad Taylor to attain his
     goal of presenting the entire Shakespearean
     canon (including *Pericles* and *Two Noble Kinsmen*)
     in three and a half years.

DATE

266 Bertram, Paul. "The Date of *The Two Noble Kinsmen*." *Shakespeare Quarterly*, 12 (1961): 21-32.

Reprint in revised form in item 233, Appendix A, pp. 283-96. Bertram settles on a date of 1613.

See also items 1, 2, 20, 26, 30, 44, 53, 237, 239, 270, 271, 273, 276, 278, 279, 280.

SOURCES

267 Thompson, Ann. "Jailers' Daughters in *The Arcadia* and *The Two Noble Kinsmen*," *Notes and Queries*, 224 (1979): 140-1.

Compares passages from *The Countess of Pembroke's Arcadia* (p. 718 in the New Penguin edition) and *The Two Noble Kinsmen* (5.2.75-9) and concludes that the former is the source of the latter. The *Arcadia* passage is a portion of a dialog between Dametas, a jailer, and Mopsa, his daughter. The passage from the play is part of a dialog between the Jailer's Daughter and her Wooer. Thompson notes that both present an apparently mad daughter obsessed with thoughts of her marriage to the point that she dismisses the possibility that her father may be hanged. There are further similarities: the girl's unrequited love for a social superior, and the reason for the father's hanging (an important prisoner has escaped). Thompson attributes 5.2 to Fletcher and reminds us that he had demonstrated knowledge of the *Arcadia* in *The Faithful Shepherdess*, *Cupid's Revenge* "and other plays" (p. 141). She finds it likely that he would have recalled it again when working on the somewhat similar subject-matter of *The Two Noble Kinsmen*.

268 Turner, Robert K., Jr. "*The Two Noble Kinsmen* and Speght's Chaucer," *Notes and Queries*, 225 (1980): 175-6.

Notes that it is generally accepted that Shakespeare and Fletcher in writing *The Two*

Noble Kinsmen drew on Speght's *Chaucer* in either the first edition of 1598 or the second edition of 1602. There is a curious reading in the second edition which suggests that it is the one that was used. In the play (4.2) three of the contending knights are described, some of the details having been adapted from the *Knight's Tale*. Of one the play says: "His head's yellow, Hard-haired and curled, thick-twined like ivy tods" (11. 103-4). Speght's 1598 edition reads: "His crispe hear lyk rings was yronne, and that was yelow" (1. 2165); the 1602 edition reads: "His crispe haire like rings was of yron," a clear mis-reading of the earlier edition. Turner concludes that the 1602 Speght rather than the 1598 edition is the source of the passage in *The Two Noble Kinsmen*, and therefore the edition the playwrights used.

See also items 2, 20, 42, 44, 213, 233, 236, 237, 245, 260, 270, 273, 276, 278, 279, 280.

TEXT AND EDITIONS

269 Farmer, John S., ed. *The Two Noble Kinsmen*.
    Tudor Facsimile Texts No. 141. Edinburgh
    and London: by the Editor, 1910. Reprint.
    New York: AMS, 1970.

    Photographic facsimile of the British Museum
    copy of the quarto of 1634.

270 Kittredge, George Lyman, ed. *The Two Noble*
    Kinsmen. *Complete Works*. Boston: Ginn,
    1936.

    The text is based on the quarto of 1634.
    Kittredge accepts Moseley's ascription to
    Fletcher and Shakespeare--"probably they worked
    in active collaboration" (p. 1409), and specu-
    lates that each made some contribution to the
    parts written by the other. He assigns 1.1,
    .2, .3 and .4; 2.1; 3.1; and 5.1, .3 and .4 to
    Shakespeare and perhaps 4.3. The main plot is
    adapted and condensed from Chaucer. The de-
    tails of the underplot are Fletcher's, but the
    general idea may have been Shakespeare's. Nei-
    ther of the earlier Palamon and Arcite plays
    are likely to have been used as sources by the
    collaborators. The date of composition is 1613
    shortly after Beaumont's masque performed at
    Whitehall in February.

271 Waller, Frederick O., ed. *A Critical, Old-Spel-*
    ling Edition of The Two Noble Kinsmen. Uni-
    versity of Chicago diss., 1957.

    Text is based on the quarto of 1634, presented in a variorum format.

Waller reviews the history of the text including discussions of the possibility that
D'Avenant in adapting the play for the Restoration stage may have had a playhouse manuscript
different from that which supplied the copy-
text for the quarto, and of the editorial
treatment of the text in earlier editions. He
accepts 1613 as the date of composition in consideration of the borrowing from Beaumont's
anti-masque, Jonson's allusion in *Bartholomew
Fair* and the mention of losses in the prolog,
supported by some peripheral evidence. Examination of linguistic characteristics clearly
shows two playwrights and that they are Shakespeare and Fletcher. Waller describes the
printing of the quarto, including identifying
the presence of two compositors, and adduces
evidence for an unusual species of copy-text.
He published his findings about the copy-text
in revised and expanded form in item 272.

272 Waller, Frederick O. "Printer's Copy for *The
     Two Noble Kinsmen*," *Studies in Bibliography*,
     11 (1958): 61-84.

Examines the 1634 quarto of *The Two Noble
Kinsmen* in an effort to determine the nature of
the copy from which the printer Waterson worked,
accepting the division of the play between two
dramatists and confirming it on the basis of
bibliographic findings. The presence of Fletcher is clear, that of Shakespeare less so.
The text exhibits unusually mixed evidence of
printer's copy. There are readily identifiable
signs of the book-keeper's hand but also equally clear signs of authorial foul papers. The
names of two actors are printed in the text who
were only associated with the King's Men in
1625-6 so Waterson's copy could not have been
the prompt book of the original production
(1613) or of the assumed revival of 1619-20.
There are a series of textual tangles which
occur exclusively in the non-Fletcherian parts
and which are only occasionally of compositorial origin. The portions of *The Two Noble Kinsmen* assigned on non-bibliographical evidence to
Fletcher display fewer of his distinctive syn-

tactical habits and spellings (e.g.: *ye*, *'em*)
than might have been anticipated in view of the
incidence of these characteristics in his other
plays. While there is evidence that the two
playwrights worked according to a plan, it is
clear that the collaboration was not a close
one and that one of the writers--most probably
Fletcher--was assigned the task of joining the
two contributions. In the course of this process, which is most evident at places where the
jointure is imperfect (e.g.: between scenes 2.1
and 2.2), Fletcher inserted a few lines into
Shakespeare's text for purposes of transition.
There is no sign of systematic revision. Waller tentatively suggests an hypothesis, ration-
alizing the apparently conflicting evidence:
the collaborators sent their individual contributions to the King's Men who found Fletcher's
pages so "messy" (p. 79) that they were transcribed. Shakespeare's part, although not perfect, was not copied. The playhouse scribe
suppressed some of Fletcher's most notable linguistic characteristics and produced copy with
virtually no cruxes. Shakespeare's sheets, not
having been reworked, exhibit some textual
tangles. The book-keeper then added his notes
to this mixed copy which may or may not have
been transcribed to provide a prompt book. On
the occasion of the revival of the mid-1620s
the book-keeper added the names of the two
minor actors and this became Waterson's copy.
Waller is well aware of the complexity of
his hypothesis and sums up: "But whether the printer's copy was an intermediate transcript, foul
papers, or a mixture of the two, it seems clear
enough that foul papers are the ultimate basis
for the quarto" (p. 80).

273 Leech, Clifford, ed. *The Two Noble Kinsmen*.
The Signet Classic Shakespeare. New York:
New American Library, 1963. Reprint. *Com-
plete Signet Classic Shakespeare*. New York:
Harcourt Brace Jovanovich, 1972. 2nd ed.,
rev. (bound with *Titus Andronicus* and
Pericles) New American Library, 1977.

A modern spelling critical edition based on

the text of the 1634 quarto.

Leech accepts the dual authorship of the play which he confirms by references to the differences of style, diction and handling of details of the plot. These are outward manifestations of two different attitudes toward the story. Shakespeare treats with high seriousness the plight of the two noble kinsmen seeing them as playthings of the gods. Fletcher recognizes the essential absurdity of the situation of the principals and treats the tale as wry comedy. While both playwrights carry forward the fundamental elements of Shakespeare's earlier romances, Shakespeare recalls *Two Gentlemen of Verona* and *A Midsummer Night's Dream* as well. Expressing some reservation on the prolog and epilog, and on 1.4 and .5, Leech assigns to Shakespeare Act 1; 2.1 ll. 1-59; 3.1; and 5.1, .3 and .4. The play in both the Shakespearean and Fletcherian parts is strongly reminiscent of Shakespeare's comedies and romances but the overall effect is that of a Fletcher play. Leech attributes this to Fletcher's having the responsibility of conflating the work of two poets, in the course of which he inserted some of his own lines into Shakespeare's part. The play is well-arranged despite the dichotomy of attitude and has a fairly tight structure. The subplot of the Jailer's Daughter parallels and reflects ironically on the plot of the knights. The writing in both parts is of a fairly high order just beneath the best in Shakespeare's greater plays. Leech sees Fletcher purposely adjusting his style and manner to Shakespeare's, although not slavishly, which accounts for the pervasive parallels and echoes of Shakespeare's work in the parts of the play which are palpably Fletcher's. This is most noteworthy in his adopting and extending the ironic and deflating attitude that Shakespeare exhibited in *Winter's Tale*. The time of composition is hardly in dispute in view of the borrowing from Beaumont's masque of February, 1613 and the allusion to Palamon in Jonson's *Bartholomew Fair* (1614). In "A Note on the Source" (pp. 187-91) Leech discusses the playwrights' adaptation of Chaucer's *Knight's Tale* which he accepts as the source of the play.

He finds that Shakespeare and Fletcher compressed the time, heightened the elements of confrontation, introduced dangers not in Chaucer, added the subplot of the Jailer's Daughter, and simplified the actions of the gods.

274 Waller, Frederick O. "The Use of Linguistic Criteria in Determining the Copy and Dates for Shakespeare's Plays," *Pacific Coast Studies in Shakespeare*. Edited by Waldo F. McNeir and Thelma N. Greenfield. Eugene: University of Oregon, 1966.

Makes passing reference to certain linguistic patterns in *The Two Noble Kinsmen*.

275 Bentley, Gerald Eades. "Eleven Shakespeare Quartos," *Princeton University Library Chronicle*, 30 (1969): 69-76.

Brief discussion of a copy of the 1634 quarto of *The Two Noble Kinsmen*.

276 Ribner, Irving, ed. *The Two Noble Kinsmen*. *The New Kittredge Shakespeares*. Waltham, Mass.: Blaisdell, 1969.

Text follows Kittredge's in his *Complete Works* of 1936 which was based on the 1634 quarto.
The evidence of Waterson's *Stationers' Register* entry and the title-page of the quarto crediting *The Two Noble Kinsmen* to Shakespeare and Fletcher are offset by its omission from the Shakespeare First Folio leaving Shakespeare's participation in the play undetermined. Paul Bertram's attempt to prove that the entire play is Shakespeare's (item 233) does not deal adequately with Waterson's attribution. Ribner accepts the scholarly consensus that Shakespeare planned the play and wrote the beginning and the ending while Fletcher wrote the middle. The date of composition is 1613. The source is Chaucer's *Knight's Tale* except for the sub-plot which the dramatists invented. In its structure and in its treatment of love, *The Two Noble Kinsmen* is unlike any of Shakespeare's plays

except *The Two Gentlemen of Verona*. In its
artificial codes of conduct, fixed moral stances and rapid changes of sentiment *The Two
Noble Kinsmen* is distinctively Fletcherian,
most closely allied to *The Maid's Tragedy*
which he wrote with Beaumont in 1610. It is a
Blackfriars play especially in its conflict
between courtly love and knightly brotherhood,
but it lacks the special qualities of Shakespeare's romances.

277   Freehafer, John. "A Textual Crux in *The Two
      Noble Kinsmen*," *English Language Notes*, 7
      (1970): 254-7.

      Cites crux at 3.4.9 in which the Jailer's
Daughter under the illusion she is seeing a
ship in danger calls out suggestions to the
sailors, including "Vpon her before the winde,
you'll loose all els:" The problem is the
first word of the line which fails to make
sense. It has been variously amended to "Up
with her," "Spoon her," "Spoom her," "Run her"
and most recently by Bertram (item 233 pp. 118-
9) to "Boom her." Except for *spoon* and *spoom*
the emendations fail to take into account the
graphic of the descender of the *p* in *Vpon*, and
the words suggested do not fit the sense of the
passage. Freehafer believes "open her" meets
the requirements of graphics, context, syntax
and topography. The compositorial misreading
is an easy substitution.

278   Proudfoot, G. R., ed. *The Two Noble Kinsmen*.
      Regents Renaissance Drama Series. Lincoln:
      University of Nebraska Press, 1970.

      A critical modern-spelling edition based on
the quarto of 1634 for which twelve copies were
collated. Press variants are noted.
      Two markedly different styles clearly point
to two different poets. Fletcher's hand is
manifest and internal evidence points to Shakespeare as the other dramatist. The collaboration must be accepted because of the positive
evidence, both external (*Stationers' Register*
entry and the quarto title-page) and internal
as adduced by Littledale in his edition of

1876-85; by A. C. Bradley ("Scene-Endings in
Shakespeare and in *The Two Noble Kinsmen*," *A
Miscellany*. London: Macmillan, 1929); by Hart
(item 5), Armstrong (item 207), Mincoff (item
215), Hoy (item 227) and others, as well as the
lack of a feasible alternative. [Proudfoot
does not allude to his earlier suggestion (item
30) of the possible presence of a third collaborator.] He assigns to Shakespeare 1; 2.1;
3.1 and .2; 4.3; and 5.1, .3 and .4. The principal source is Chaucer's *Knight's Tale*, but
numerous details are traced to North's *Plutarch*,
Boccaccio's *Teseida*, Statius's *Thebais*, Sidney's
Lady of May, Beaumont's *Masque of the Inner Temple and Gray's Inn*, Fletcher's *Coxcomb* and
Shakespeare's *Love's Labor's Lost*, *Midsummer
Night's Dream*, *Hamlet* and *Pericles*. No source
for the subplot has been identified and probably none exists. The theme of *The Two Noble
Kinsmen* is the bitterness and destructive power
of love. The thematic conflict is well worked
out in the beginning and ending but the central
portion of the play dealing with the love-rival-
ry of Palamon and Arcite does not seem to bear
any essential relationship to the broad theme.
The need for suspense until the denouement im-
poses a difficulty which Fletcher did not satis-
factorily resolve. The impressiveness of *The
Two Noble Kinsmen* lies in its mastery of tragicomic effects and in its exploration of the in-
scrutability of the gods and the dangerous power
of love. The use of Beaumont's anti-masque and
the reference in *Bartholomew Fair* establish
a date in the late summer of 1613.

279 Smith, Hallett, ed. *The Two Noble Kinsmen*.
     The Riverside Shakespeare. Boston: Houghton
     Mifflin, 1974. Pp. 1639-81.

     A modern spelling critical edition based on
the 1634 quarto.
     Smith finds that *The Two Noble Kinsmen* is a
collaboration based primarily on the external
evidence (Waterson's attribution in *Stationers'
Register* and on the title-page of the quarto).
Studies of metrical characteristics, vocabulary,
word compounding, contractions, imagery and
verse enable scholars to divide the play with

some but not complete confidence. A consensus
assigns to Shakespeare Act 1 (except the opening song); 2.1; 3.1; 5.1 ll. 34-173, .3 and .4.
Two scenes, 1.4 and .5, are uncertain and the
prolog and epilog are given to Fletcher. The
date of composition is 1613 and the source is
Chaucer's *Knight's Tale*, to which the collaborators added the sub-plot of the Jailer's
Daughter. Shakespeare's scenes are marked by
characteristic imagery, rhetoric (the three
prayers in 5.1), and theatrical spectacle (the
opening scene). The play deals in a curious
way with the themes of innocence and experience,
of innocence in the midst of corruption, of the
failure of the will of the characters to be
effective. There are many links between *The
Two Noble Kinsmen* and the other romances, all
of which are well suited to the tastes of the
Blackfriars audience for whom they were written.

280 Bawcutt, N. W., ed. *The Two Noble Kinsmen*.
    New Penguin Shakespeare. Harmondsworth:
    Penguin, 1977.

    Modern spelling critical text based on the
    quarto of 1634.
    Scholarly opinion in the past 40 years, aided
    by increasingly sophisticated authorship tests,
    has moved in the direction of accepting the
    Stationers' Register and title page ascription
    to Fletcher and Shakespeare. This external evi-
    dence for collaboration is supported by stylis-
    tic considerations. We can only speculate as
    to why it was excluded from the Shakespeare
    First Folio. Perhaps there were copyright prob-
    lems, or the manuscript may have been mislaid
    or it may have been omitted because less than
    half of it is Shakespeare's. The main source
    is Chaucer's *Knight's Tale*. Subsidiary sources
    include Beaumont's second anti-masque from his
    Masque of the Inner Temple and Gray's Inn which
    "has no organic function and could ... be omitted
    as in fact it was in the York Festival produc-
    tion ... in 1973" (p. 16); echoes of *Love's
    Labor's Lost*, *A Midsummer Night's Dream* and
    Hamlet; and Sidney's *Lady of May* for a comic
    schoolmaster. The sub-plot is an invention of

Fletcher's. A sympathetic reading of the play, an understanding of its stylistic qualities and an unbiased assessment of what the authors were trying to accomplish (a dual portrait of true nobility in a setting disturbed by conflicts of love) leads to the conclusion that Shakespeare and Fletcher were trying to say something of value.

Index

INDEX

References are to item numbers

Acts and Monuments
(Foxe), 50, 118, 160,
171
Agate, James, 206
A Larum for London
(anon.), 58, 97
Alexander, Peter, 31,
169, 201, 215, 217
Alice Pierce (anon.), 7
*All's Well That Ends
Well*, 24
Andreas, James, 263
Antony and Cleopatra, 5,
39, 227
Arcadia (Sidney), 267
Arcite, 30, 35, 43, 46,
202, 203, 213, 215,
222, 230, 233, 236,
241, 248, 249, 250,
252, 253, 257, 261,
264, 278
Armstrong, Edward A.,
20, 25, 207, 219, 278
Armstrong, R. L., 90,
94
Armstrong, William A.,
91
*Arraignment of Paris,
The* (Peele), 76
As You Like It, 27
Auden, W. H., 246

Bald, R. C., 31, 99,
111, 146, 148, 181
Baldwin, T. W., 70

Barnet, Sylvan, 36
Barroll, J. Leeds, 176
Bartholomew Fair (Jon-
son), 1, 2, 44, 233,
273, 278
Bates, Merete, 249
*Battaile of Agincourt,
The* (Drayton), 61
Battle of Alcazar, The
(Peele), 76
Baugh, Albert C., 12
Bawcutt, N. W., 280
Beaumont, Francis, 1, 2,
8, 9, 14, 26, 39, 43,
44, 45, 186, 194, 197,
201, 211, 215, 216,
227, 233, 236, 241,
258, 270, 271, 273,
276, 278, 280
Beebe, Richard, 178
Bentley, Gerald Eades,
11, 21, 132, 189, 275
Bergeron, David M., 135
Berkowitz, Gerald M., 264
Bertram, Paul, 30, 31,
233, 238, 239, 241, 266,
276, 277
Bethell, S. L., 67, 211
Betterton, Thomas, 194
Bevington, David, 81
*Bibliographical evidence
of authorship*, 23, 29,
31, 32, 47, 51, 53, 55,
56, 92, 95, 100, 108,
124, 131, 134, 167, 171,

177, 178, 179, 181,
233, 241, 271, 272
Birth of Merlin, The,
(Rowley), 4
Black, Ben Wathen, 170
Black Prince (char-
acter), 13, 74
Blayney, Peter M. W., 133
Boat on the Serchio
(Shelley), 25
Book of Martyrs
(Foxe). *See Acts and
Monuments*
Bradbrook, M. C., 37,
43, 66, 126, 138, 244,
258
Bradford, Gamaliel, 24,
197
Bradley, A. C., 278
Brinkmann, Karl, 127
Brockbank, Philip, 184
Brooke, C. F. Tucker,
12, 20, 50, 151, 163,
167, 173, 181, 243
Brown, John Russell,
30, 235
Brownists, 153, 154,
155
Brownlow, F. W., 257

Cadwalader, John, 187
Cairncross, A. S., 77
Camden, Carroll, 229
Campbell, Oscar James,
28
Candido, Joseph, 147
Capell, Edward, 31, 94
Captain Thomas Stukeley
(anon.) 85
Captives, The (Hey-
wood), 101, 144
Cardinal Wolsey (1: Chet-
tle, Drayton, Munday
and Smith; 2: Chettle),
113
Castle, Eduard, 186
Chambers, E. K., 2,
113, 159, 175

Chambers, R. W., 2, 20,
95, 103, 105, 107, 109,
111, 113, 136, 141, 151,
179
Chambrun, Clara Long-
worth de, 10, 104
Chapman, George, 2, 111
Chaucer, Geoffrey, 2, 20,
44, 50, 213, 214, 233,
247, 257, 260, 263, 268,
273, 276, 278, 279, 280
Chettle, Henry, 26, 102,
117, 124, 133, 144, 146
Chillington, Carol A.,
146
Clayton, Thomas, 32, 176,
182
Clemen, Wolfgang, 127
Clements, Robert Morrison,
Jr., 255
Cobbler's Prophecy, The
(Wilson), 58
Collins, D. C., 146, 152
Comedy of Errors, The,
221
Coriolanus, 5, 39, 105,
109, 124, 136, 158, 161,
184, 207
Cornelia (Kyd), 73
*Countess of Pembroke's
Arcadia. See Arcadia*
Countess of Salisbury
(character), 13, 50, 74,
79, 85
Coxcomb, The (Fletcher),
278
Crawford, Charles, 88
Crundell, H. W., 61, 106,
154
Cupid's Revenge (Flet-
cher), 267
Cutts, John P., 236
Cymbeline, 11, 35, 39, 43,
215, 217, 226, 228, 234,
247

Damon and Pithias (Ed-
wardes), 245

Davenant, Sir William,
  19, 188, 194, 242, 271
David and Bethsabe
  (Peele), 76
Dawson, Giles E., 47,
  185
Dayton Daily News, 220
Dekker, Thomas, 26, 117,
  124, 133, 144, 146,
  152, 158, 159, 163
De Quincey, Thomas, 243
Deutschberger, Paul,
  109
Digges, Leonard, 233,
  241
Dobson, Willis B., 69
Doctor Faustus (Mar-
  lowe), 130
Don Quixote (tr. Shel-
  ton), 2, 20, 40, 186,
  194, 196, 197
Doran, Madeleine, 108
Double Falsehood. See
  Section IV, *Cardenio*
Downes, John, 194
Drayton, Michael, 61,
  62
Dyce, Alexander, 50,
  52, 163, 168, 171,
  173

Eagles, R. L., 153
Edmund Ironside (anon.),
  15, 17, 25, 140
Edward I (Peele), 76
Edward II (Marlowe), 10, 13
Edward III (character),
  13, 74, 79, 81, 83, 84,
  85
Edwardes, Richard, 245
Edwards, Philip, 230,
  237, 240, 260
Eliot, T. S., 243
Ellis-Fermor, Una, 31,
  130, 211, 226
Emilia (character), 30,
  43, 202, 213, 226, 230,
  233, 236, 241, 248,

  250, 252, 253
*England's Heroical
  Epistles* (Drayton),
  61, 62
Erdman, David V., 29, 111
Escapes of Jupiter, The
  (Heywood), 101
Evans, G. Blakemore, 55,
  56, 181
Everitt, E. B., 15, 25, 90

Fair Em (anon.), 97
*Fair Maid of the West,
  The* (Heywood), 85
Faithful Friends, The
  (Fletcher), 194
Faithful Shepherdess, The
  (Fletcher), 267
Farjeon, Herbert, 52
Farmer, John S., 7, 87,
  162, 181, 269
Feuillerat, Albert, 114
*First Part of the Con-
  tention betwixt the two
  famous Houses of York
  and Lancaster, The*
  (anon.), 77
Fisher, John, Bishop of
  Rochester (character),
  137
Fletcher, John, 1, 2, 3,
  6, 8, 9, 11, 12, 14, 16,
  18, 19, 20, 21, 24, 26,
  28, 29, 30, 34, 35, 39,
  41, 42, 43, 44, 45, 49,
  50, 186, 188, 194, 196,
  197, 201, 202, 205, 211,
  214, 215, 216, 217, 218,
  227, 233, 239, 241, 245,
  256, 267, 270, 271, 272,
  273, 276, 278, 280
Foakes, R. A., 18
Fogel, Ephim G., 23, 29,
  111
Forker, Charles R., 147
Frazier, Harriet C., 192,
  193, 195, 196
Freehafer, John, 40, 194,

277
Freeman, Arthur, 80
Froissart, Jean, 2, 20,
  50, 78, 90
Frye, Northrop, 259

Gaskell, Philip, 134
Gildon, Charles, 194
Golding, S. R., 58, 97
Graham, Walter, 186,
  197
Granville-Barker, Har-
  ley, 164
Greene, Robert, 2, 5,
  59, 75
Greenfield, Thelma N.,
  274
Greg, W. W., 2, 16, 20,
  51, 52, 95, 96, 100,
  111, 113, 123, 124,
  141, 144, 163, 166,
  167, 171, 173, 181,
  183
Griffin, Alice, 225
Grivelet, Michel, 82

Hall, Edward, 50, 160,
  171
Halliday, F. E., 19, 218
Hamlet, 14, 39, 99, 117,
  136, 198, 253, 278,
  280
Harbage, Alfred, 33,
  188, 209, 214
Harris, Bernard, 30, 235
Harrison, G. B., 152,
  164
Hart, Alfred, 5, 31, 78,
  94, 278
Hartwig, Joan, 247
Hays, Michael L., 47,
  139, 183
Heminges, John and Henry
  Condell, 34, 51, 212, 233
Henning, Standish, 143
Henry IV (1 and 2), 5,
  7, 63, 99, 117, 121,
  122, 136, 207

Henry V, 5, 7, 14, 20,
  43, 66, 71, 99, 122,
  125, 136, 185, 207
Henry VI (1, 2 and 3),
  5, 10, 14, 43, 71, 77,
  84, 86, 88, 105, 184
Henry VIII, 1, 6, 8, 9,
  10, 11, 14, 18, 24, 30,
  35, 39, 50, 51, 127,
  211, 212, 215, 217,
  218, 226, 227, 233,
  245, 247
Hero and Leander (Mar-
  lowe), 2
Heywood, Thomas, 26, 101,
  113, 119, 124, 133, 144,
  146, 152
Hickson, Samuel, 31, 233
Hippolyta (character),
  220, 226
Hobday, C. H., 27
Holinshed, Raphael, 48,
  50, 78, 90, 91
Honigmann, E. A. J., 175
Hosley, Richard, 48
Howard, Tony, 261
Howard-Hill, T. H., 182
Howarth, R. G., 75
Hoy, Cyrus, 79, 227, 233,
  241, 278
Huber, R. A., 47, 123,
  141
Hunter, G. K., 140
Hyde, Mary C., 116, 221

Imagery, 20, 25, 27, 31,
  38, 40, 43, 71, 76, 95,
  98, 136, 143, 144, 181,
  207, 215, 226, 227, 279

Jackson, B. A. W., 123
Jackson, MacD. P., 25, 77,
  92, 159, 174, 178, 179
Jacobs, Henry E., 45
Jailer's Daughter (char-
  acter), 30, 35, 43, 44,
  45, 46, 199, 206, 214,
  220, 229, 230, 243, 247,

250, 257, 265, 267,
273, 277
James IV (Greene), 59,
75
Jenkins, Harold, 31,
102, 124, 151, 167,
171
Jewkes, Wilfred T., 53
*John a Kent and John
a Cumber* (Munday), 2,
102, 140, 178
John of Bordeaux
(anon.), 102
Jones, M. G., 231
Jonson, Ben, 1, 2, 111
Jorgensen, Paul A.,
222
Joseph, Sr. Miriam,
210
Julius Caesar, 27, 65,
105, 106, 111, 136,
150, 184, 215

Kay, Carol McGinnis,
45
Kermode, Frank, 35,
228
Kimbrough, Robert, 140
Kind Heart's Dream
(Chettle), 133
King and No King, A,
(Beaumont and Flet-
cher), 79, 241
King John, 5, 14, 65,
136
King Lear, 106, 117,
125, 136, 149, 150,
161, 207, 215, 251
Kittridge, George Lyman,
239, 270, 276
Knight's Tale (Chaucer),
2, 20, 44, 50, 213,
214, 233, 247, 257,
260, 263, 268, 273,
276, 278, 279, 280
Knowles, Richard, 140
Kökeritz, Helge, 208
Koskenniemi, Inna, 76

Kozlenko, William, 93
Kyd, Thomas, 25, 59, 63,
73, 76, 80

Lady of May, The (Sidney),
278, 280
Lake, D. J., 158, 159
Lambrechts, G., 73, 76,
80
Lane, Ralph H., 121
Lapidas, Fred, 94
Law, Robert Adger, 17,
101
Leech, Clifford, 11, 24,
37, 45, 202, 230, 243,
273
Leek, Robert - H., 145
Lewis, John S., 85
Leyris, Pierre, 243
Lindabury, Richard J., 60
Linguistic evidence of
authorship, 2, 3, 5, 15,
20, 26, 29, 31, 32, 39,
40, 47, 59, 63, 65, 95,
105, 117, 121, 122, 124,
130, 133, 143, 148, 150,
151, 159, 172, 181, 185,
194, 204, 210, 214, 226,
227, 233, 241, 243, 271,
273, 274, 279, 280
Littledale, Harold, 31,
40, 50, 278
Livermore, Ann, 129
Lodowick, 83
Long, William B., 142
Love's Labor's Lost, 20,
278, 280
Love's Labor's Won, 55
Lusty Juventus (Wever),
147, 171

Maas, Paul, 115
Macbeth, 39, 99, 136,
207, 215, 242, 243
Macdonell, A. G., 199
Mackail, John W., 3
MacNalty, Arthur Salus-
bury, 122

Mad Lover, The (Fletcher), 227
Maid's Tragedy, The (Beaumont and Fletcher), 276
Malcontent, The (Marston), 79
Marder, Louis, 148
Margeson, J. M. R., 37
Marlowe, Christopher, 2, 5, 25, 59, 88, 111
Marriage of Wit and Wisdom, The (anon.), 147
Masque elements, 1, 2, 30, 43, 44, 45, 224, 233, 236, 244, 255, 258, 259, 263
Masque of the Inner Temple and Gray's Inn (Beaumont), 1, 2, 43, 44, 45, 233, 236, 237, 258, 273, 278, 280
Massinger, Philip, 1, 2, 8, 50, 189, 197, 215
Matchett, William H., 143
Maxwell, Baldwin, 8, 118
Maxwell, J. C., 92
McMillan, Scott, 177
McNeir, Waldo F., 274
Measure for Measure, 20, 43, 65, 89
Merchant of Venice, The, 85, 121, 135, 143
Meres, Francis, 125
Merriam, Thomas, 148, 150, 151
Merry Wives of Windsor, The, 207, 273
Metamorphoses (Ovid), 82
Metrical evidence of authorship, 2, 3, 20, 29, 31, 32, 47, 50, 59, 71, 181, 194, 201, 202, 217, 233, 241, 279

Metz, G. Harold, 151
Midsummer Night's Dream, A, 121, 263, 278, 280
Mincoff, M., 31, 211, 215, 278
Monsieur Thomas (Fletcher), 217
More, Sir Thomas (character), 43, 103, 122, 137, 171
More Dissemblers Besides Women (Middleton), 236
Morris dance. *See* Masque elements
Moseley, Humphrey, 1, 16, 24, 34, 56, 186, 188, 189, 194
Mucedorus (anon.), 245
Much Ado About Nothing, 121
Muir, Kenneth, 20, 25, 31, 39, 46, 49, 55, 68, 76, 78, 83, 190, 191, 219, 223, 226, 233, 244, 245, 252
Munday, Anthony, 26, 100, 117, 122, 124, 125, 135, 146, 174, 178, 183
Munro, John, 173

Nicoll, Allardyce, 224, 237
Nosworthy, J. M., 20, 31, 119, 130, 151

O'Connor, Frank, 65, 94
Oliphant, E. H. C., 1, 2, 4, 31, 197
Onions, C. T., 155
Oras, Ants, 217
Osterberg, V., 59
Othello, 99, 136, 143, 215, 253

Painter, William, 2, 20, 50, 59, 78, 90, 91
Palace of Pleasure, The (Painter), 20, 59, 90

Palamon, 30, 35, 43, 46,
  199, 202, 203, 213,
  214, 215, 220, 230,
  233, 236, 241, 246,
  248, 249, 250, 252,
  253, 257, 261, 262,
  264, 278
Palamon and Arcite
  (anon.), 26
Paleographic evidence
  of authorship, 2, 9,
  14, 31, 47, 95, 96,
  109, 111, 114, 121,
  122, 125, 139, 141,
  144, 157, 172, 181,
  182
Parrott, Thomas M., 6
Partridge, A. C., 26,
  212
Pedlar's Prophecy, The
  (anon.), 97
Peele, George, 2, 5,
  20, 63
Pericles, 1, 2, 14, 16,
  35, 40, 51, 150, 194,
  211, 226, 228, 234,
  236, 245, 247, 278
Petronella, Vincent F.,
  253
Pettet, E. C., 213
Petti, Anthony G., 144
Philaster (Beaumont
  and Fletcher), 39, 241
Pirithous, 43, 230
Plutarch's Lives (tr.
  North), 278
Pollard, A. W., **9**, 20,
  95, 111, 124, 141, 165
Pope, Alexander, 1, 243
Proudfoot, G. R., 30,
  40, 57, 278
Purves, Alan C., 202,
  204

Quinn, Edward G., 28

Rabkin, Norman, 238,
  256

Ramsey, Paul, 47, 141
Rape of Lucrece, The, 2,
  20, 65, 71, 76, 198
*Rare Triumphs of Love and
  Fortune, The* (anon.),
  43, 245
Reese, Gertrude C., 64
Reese, M. M., 14, 72
Revenger's Tragedy, The
  (anon.), 79
Ribner, Irving, 78, 276
Richard II, 5, 20, 27,
  82, 99, 105, 136, 191,
  194
Richard III, 14, 27, 122
Riggs, David, 84
Rivals, The (Davenant),
  19, 242
Robertson, John, 31, 63
Rochester, Bishop of
  (character). *See*
  Fisher, John
Romeo and Juliet, 27,
  198, 215
Rowley, Samuel, 2
Ruoff, James E., 41

Salisbury, Earl of (char-
  acter), 13, 85
Sarrazin, G., 63
Scarlet, Thomas, 94
Schevill, Rudolph, 186,
  197
Schoenbaum, S., 22, 31,
  32, 34, 42, 47, 55, 244,
  245
Schücking, Levin L., 31,
  113
Schütt, Marie, 160
Schwartzstein, Leonard,
  198
*Second Maiden's Tragedy,
  The* (anon.), 15
Seltzer, Daniel, 235
Shakespeare Memorial
  Library, Birmingham, 120
Shapiro, I. A., 20, 102,
  125, 156

Sharpe, Robert Boies, 7
Shelley, Percy B., 25
Shirley, Frances A., 262
Shirley, John, 166
Sir Clyamon and Sir
   Clamydes (anon.), 43
Sir John Oldcastle
   (Drayton, Munday, Hath-
   away and Wilson), 13,
   97, 173
Sir John van Olden
   Barnavelt (Fletcher
   and Massinger), 194
Sisson, C. J., 31, 123,
   211
Smith, G. C. Moore, 88,
   91
Smith, Hallett, 234,
   239, 248, 279
Smith, Irwin, 232
Smith, R. M., 90
Soliman and Perseda
   (Kyd), 73, 76
Sonnets (Shakespeare),
   6, 7, 43, 65, 82
Spalding, William, 31,
   233
Spanish Tragedy, The
   (Kyd), 4, 71, 73, 76
Spencer, Christopher,
   242
Spencer, Hazleton, 9
Spencer, T. J. B., 237
Spencer, Theodore,
   202, 204, 205
Spenser, Edmund, 25
Spevack, Marvin, 54
Spikes, Judith Doolin,
   137
Spurgeon, Caroline F. E.,
   20, 31, 98, 102
Stage and Television
   Today, 250
Stage history, Double
   Falsehood, 196; Sir
   Thomas More, 100, 116,
   117, 122, 126, 130,
   138, 140, 145, 163,

171, 177; The Two Noble
   Kinsmen, 199, 206, 220,
   221, 224, 225, 231, 232,
   235, 249, 250, 254, 261,
   264, 265, 280
Stirling, Brents, 112
Stoddard, Joseph H., 265
Styan, J. L., 128
Style as evidence of
   authorship. See Lin-
   guistic evidence of
   authorship
Swinburne, A. C., 243
Sykes, H. D., 63

Talbert, Ernest William,
   74
Taming of a Shrew, The,
   207
Taming of the Shrew, The,
   14, 27, 207
Tannenbaum, Samuel A.,
   9, 14, 16, 31, 101, 119
Tempest, The, 3, 5, 11,
   35, 39, 50, 207, 217,
   224, 228, 234, 238, 247,
   248
Teseida (Boccaccio), 278
Textual evidence of
   authorship. See Bibliographical evidence of
   authorship
Thebais (Statius), 278
Theobald, Lewis, 1, 2, 24,
   30, 40, 50, 186, 187,
   188, 191, 192, 193, 194,
   196, 197
Theseus, 43, 213, 218,
   230, 233, 253, 257, 259,
   262, 263
Thomas Lord Cromwell
   (anon.), 113, 118, 173
Thomas of Woodstock
   (anon.), 140
Thompson, Ann, 260, 267
Thompson, Sir E. Maunde,
   20, 95, 109, 111, 123,
   141, 181

Thorndike, A. H., 1
*Three Lords and Three
Ladies of London*
(Wilson), 58
Tillotson, Kathleen, 62
Tillyard, E. M. W., 13,
72
Tilney, Edmund, 2, 133,
163
Timon of Athens, 14, 39,
40, 130, 136, 211, 226,
227, 257
Titus Andronicus, 150
Tobias, Richard T., 252
Tourneur, Cyril, 2
Trewin, J. C., 254
Troilus and Cressida,
40, 99, 105, 109, 111,
117, 136, 161, 227,
233, 253
*Troublesome Reign of King
John, The* (anon.), 63
*True Tragedy of Richard
Duke of York, The*
(anon.), 77
Turner, Robert K., Jr.,
268
Twelfth Night, 40
*Two Gentlemen of Verona,
The*, 20, 89, 135, 243,
273, 276
Tyrrell, Henry, 93

Ure, Peter, 245
Urkowitz, Steven, 149

Vancura, Zdenek, 211
VanDoren, Mark, 203
Venus and Adonis, 20, 71
Versification. *See*
Metrical evidence of
authorship
Very Woman, A (Massin-
ger), 8, 189
Villiers, 13, 85
Vocabulary. *See* Lin-
guistic evidence of
authorship

Waith, Eugene M., 216
Waller, Frederick O.,
30, 227, 233, 271, 272,
274
Walton, J. K., 131
Warburton, John, 1
Warnke, K. and L.
Proescholdt, 50
Warwick, Earl of
(character), 13, 50, 85
Waterson, John, 41, 215,
227, 272, 276, 279
Webster, John, 146
Wells, Stanley, 40, 237
Wells, William, 63
Wentersdorf, Karl P., 38,
71, 77, 86, 94, 136,
157, 180
Wickham, Glynne, 251
Wilds, Lillian, 265
Willoughby, Edwin Eliott,
164
Wilson, F. P., 161
Wilson, J. Dover, 2, 20,
95, 111, 141, 172
Wilson, Robert, 58, 97
Winny, James, 89
Winter's Tale, The, 3, 5,
11, 35, 39, 50, 204,
217, 226, 228, 233, 234,
247, 248, 273
Woman's Prize, The (Flet-
cher), 227
Women Pleased (Fletcher),
227
Wyatt, Sir Thomas, 71

Zalbrod, Paul G., 252
Zelauto (Munday), 135
Zesmer, David M., 44